To my friend, Tommy –
with best wishes for a
Happy Birthday !
Doug Williams

So Many Summer Fields

creating friendships while connecting to baseball's past

By
Douglas Williams

authorHOUSE™

1663 LIBERTY DRIVE, SUITE 200
BLOOMINGTON, INDIANA 47403
(800) 839-8640
WWW.AUTHORHOUSE.COM

First published by AuthorHouse 10/17/05

ISBN: 1-4208-8801-3 (sc)

Library of Congress Control Number: 2005908892

Printed in the United States of America
Bloomington, Indiana

This book is printed on acid-free paper.

Cover photo by George Pongratz. Items shown include: shoes and cap of Joe Sewell, wire photo of George Kelly, Buck Marrow matchbook cover, photos of Bud Metheny and Ray Murray and a Hank Foiles model catcher's mitt.

To My Parents,
With Love and Gratitude

ACKNOWLEDGMENTS

I gratefully acknowledge the assistance, patience, and encouragement of so many individuals who, as a whole, make it obvious that this project was meant to be. Foremost, my deepest heartfelt gratitude goes to Susan Pongratz for all her many hours of hard work and undying enthusiasm. I am also grateful to her husband, George Pongratz, for his efforts and support. Likewise, thanks to Gwen Johnson who lit the fuse to get it all underway. Sincere honor and appreciation are felt and directed to all of the former baseball players and their families who so graciously opened their homes, their lives, and their hearts to me—those who are subjects within this book as well as those who could not be included. Thanks to all of you for your time, kindness, and generosity. Finally, special thanks are extended to Swallow Turn Music Company for permission to use their lyrics for the title of the book, to The Topps Company for license to reproduce their beautiful, old cards, and to Major League Baseball for their cooperation with any team trademarks that are pictured.

Table of Contents

Preface

"Whoever would know the mind and heart of America had better learn baseball."

-- Jacques Barzun

As a teenager in the late 60s, my behavior was such that my parents must have frequently questioned themselves, wondering where they had failed. Surely they must have had their share of doubts about me, their youngest, as to what type of adult I would one day become. Interactions during that period between me and my parents frequently related to things like the length of my hair, how late I was out the night before, or the loud volume of my music. My father always addressed those matters with me in his typically soft, but firm manner. He was always a patient and loving father, slow to anger. But there were many times he and I just did not see eye to eye! I never doubted his love for me. We were just up against something known as a "generation gap." Thanks to my father's patience, love, and unfailing dedication, as well as his confidence in me, we soundly defeated this opponent, the generation gap, after a few years.

But during those years when I was being my most difficult self, Dad and I were always capable of dropping our opposing issues in order to talk about baseball. The tone at the supper table could convert instantly from uneasy silence to an active dialogue of shared interest and connection.

Baseball was our common ground. On the subject of baseball, we would always listen to what the other had to say and opinions were respected. That's the magic of baseball. As Walt Whitman wrote about America's game, "It will bind us together and heal our wounds."

In many cases, Dad initiated the discussion by volunteering a bit of information from the morning newspaper. "I saw where the Orioles beat the Senators again last night."

A comment like that was all that was needed. He had taken a step towards me in a attempt to share time with me. The subject was now one of my favorites.

"Yes, sir, but Washington is getting better and besides, Baltimore still can't handle the Red Sox."

Now I in turn, had taken a step in his direction, and we were on that common ground—the verbal ball diamond. Dad would sometimes offer the same opinions I had heard many times before. But that was allowed because it was baseball.

"Brooks Robinson is one of the finest third basemen ever!" Or "Lou Brock is very well spoken and yet humble." Or "Elston Howard has the strongest throw to second base of any catcher." And the one I remember the most, "I really admire Bobby Richardson, not just for being a wonderful player, but also because he is such a dedicated Christian, who is not ashamed to share his faith with others."

Those were special times of connection with my father, times I cherish, times I miss.

My purpose for writing this book is in part to reconnect to those times. Several of the former players featured in this book were in their athletic heyday years before I was born, but at a time when my dad could have noticed any of their names in the daily sports section or heard a mention of one of them on the radio. Then, too, some of these men were just about his age. And at times, when visiting one, I would hear an expression or see a gesture that was familiar and reminiscent of my father.

There also is a compelling urge to perpetuate the legacies of each of these gracious men. Each of them received me warmly into his home. Each was friendly and accommodating with his own unique stories to share. All were pleased to be reminded that there are older fans out there who remember them and younger fans who are learning their names and stories for the first time. To me, their stories are far too precious to risk losing.

Finally, there is this self-promoting, almost boastful, need I have just to let everyone know how fortunate and blessed I am to have met these people, and in some cases, developed continuing friendships with them. Of course, I am always excited and proud to tell someone that a friend of mine is an ex-major leaguer. Years ago, I would have never thought that could happen.

Baseball has worked its magic on me throughout my life. Collecting cards and autographs, writing letters, attending games at various ballparks, all have put me in contact with so many wonderful people. Baseball is more than a sport. It is history, people, and tradition. Terrence Mann, in the movie, *Field of Dreams*, said, "Baseball represents what is good about America." Surely he was in mind of the players, the personalities, the heroes—the people. Those comprise the most valuable part of my collection, my collection of people, a collection of friends and heroes.

Douglas Williams
2005

CHAPTER 1

The Thin Man

"It would be difficult to conceive of a finer example of true sport."
- Calvin Coolidge

In 1937 Franklin D. Roosevelt was president. As our nation's economy continued to squirm its way out of the grip of the Great Depression, the technological pride of Hitler's Nazi Germany, the Zeppelin *Hindenburg* exploded and crashed at Lakehurst, New Jersey, killing 36 of 97 on board on May 6, 1937.

During that same time, however, baseball was the all-American pastime with a constellation of stars such as Lou Gehrig, Hank Greenberg, and Jimmie Foxx. In July, the sparkling career of St. Louis Cardinal pitcher Dizzy Dean was effectively ended at the All-Star game in Washington, D.C. During that game, Dean's toe was fractured by a line drive off the bat of Cleveland slugger Earl Averill. Dizzy was never again the colorful, dominating pitcher he was prior to that injury. That same year, the powerful New York Yankees defeated the then New York Giants in the World Series four games to one. But of more importance to me, it was March 27, 1937, that my father, Stanley Edward Williams, and my mother, Clarice Craig Bunting, were married. Their marriage proved to be just the opening chapter of a beautiful love story that would continue until my father's death some 54 years later.

It was with the Philadelphia Phillies that Earl "Thin Man" Allen made his major league debut in the latter part of the 1937 baseball season. Allen's nickname had much to do with his physical dimensions. Standing 6'1" and weighing 165 lbs., he presented a long and lanky physique. The nickname was undoubtedly trendy because of the popularity of *The Thin Man* movie series starring William Powell and Myrna Loy, who were two of the great entertainment headliners of the 1930s.

Allen spent almost his entire baseball career as a pitcher for various minor league teams throughout the South. It was his accuracy and fastball that caught the eye of Phillies manager Jimmy Wilson, who was responsible for having Earl signed to a major league deal with the Philadelphia Phillies. Wilson, a seasoned player, had a lot of years as a catcher with the Cardinals and Phillies. He was certainly qualified to be a judge of talent and could recognize potential in a young pitcher when he saw it.

The Phillies of '37 furnished manager Wilson with very few high quality players. The team would go on to finish a dismal 34 ½ games behind the league champions, the New York Giants of Bill Terry. Nonetheless, this was still the major leagues for 22-year-old Earl Allen.

*Earl Allen pitched for several
minor league teams throughout
the South during the 1930s.*

In the late summer of 2002, I finally decided I had waited long enough to try to get in contact with Mr. Allen. His residence in Chesapeake, Virginia, was not far from my own home, making an in-person encounter a strong possibility. After hunting phone numbers in one of the local area phone directories that matched the address I had for Mr. Allen in my baseball address book, my sleuthing proved productive, and I had the number. All I needed was to push myself to place the call.

Phoning someone I have never met is daunting. I am not so bold that I don't worry about disturbing someone or infringing on cherished privacy, especially when it involves an elderly person. In addition, many people are not receptive to receiving phone calls from strangers requesting a visit. But, thinking of the possibilities that could result by calling, I dialed.

Mrs. Allen answered, and cheerfully verified that I did indeed have the residence of *the* Earl Allen, the former Phillies' pitcher.

"Mrs. Allen, I am two hours from your home, and I was hoping I could visit Mr. Allen to get an autograph."

"Thank you for your call, but my husband honors autograph requests that he receives by mail."

"Yes, ma'am. I understand. In fact, I have often collected autographs in that way. But, since I'm so close by, I thought I could just stop by for a quick visit and meet Mr. Allen."

With some reticence, Mrs. Allen agreed. "Please remember, though, that my husband is 88-years-old and he no longer hears as well as he used to. Also, his memory is not as clear."

"Now we have family coming to visit next week, so that won't be a good time," she continued. "But call back after that, and if Earl is feeling okay, I am sure he wouldn't mind your visit."

I called her back a week later, and we made arrangements for me to visit after work.

The drive to Chesapeake, Virginia, was no easy task. The oppressive Tidewater humidity on that sultry summer day was only one of many obstacles. Rush hour traffic created waves of stationary clusters on the road. I was late by more than 30 minutes. And promptness is something I strive for.

While sitting in the traffic, I riffled through the Baseball Encyclopedia to sharpen my memory on dates and stats that would connect to Mr. Allen's brief career. I wanted to give Mr. Allen the impression I was knowledgeable about some of his teammates as well as a few of his contemporary opponents throughout the National League.

Upon my arrival at the Allens' home, I was immediately offered Southern hospitality that provided a welcomed and cool respite from the hot drive. Mrs. Allen led me to the family room, where Mr. Allen relaxed in an easy chair. After quick introductions, we shook hands.

"Mr. Allen, thank you for allowing me to visit today. I have been researching your career. Finally getting to meet you is a highlight for me." I said. "My father was born in 1913, one year before you were born," I continued. "It means a great deal to meet one of his contemporaries. I lost my best friend when my dad died 11 years ago."

"He must have been a great man to have made such a great impression on his son," Mr. Allen observed. "Tell me about him."

"Oh, my father was the best. He would always encourage me to tell him if I ever got into trouble. He would say, 'I don't care what it is all about, Doug. I will always be on your side and I will always help you, but I can't help you if I don't know about it.'"

Mr. Allen nodded. "My father was the same way, except my father claimed that he would not back me up if I were to get into trouble for stealing. He had no use for a thief."

Mr. Allen was just a teenager at the start of the Great Depression. This was a time when jobs were nearly impossible to find, especially for young boys still going to school. Sports and other organized school activities then, like today, kept many students out of trouble, pointing them in the right direction.

"Back when I was a young boy in Tennessee," he continued "a lot of kids were into stealing because times were really hard in those days. The boys who got into trouble couldn't play sports at school. Some were expelled. I think baseball helped keep me out of trouble," he reflected.

"Mr. Allen, if I recall, the '37 Phillies had some power hitters in the lineup and finished with over 100 home runs for the year. But there was quite a bit of talent on that pitching staff as well. I'd like to hear about some of your fellow pitchers for the Phillies."

Mr. Allen smiled. "There was Hugh Mulcahy, nicknamed 'Losing Pitcher' by the newspaper reporters. It seems he was constantly being credited with a defeat in the box scores in spite of consistently turning in impressive pitching performances."

"Wasn't Mulcahy an All-Star pitcher for the National League?"

"Well done, young man," Mr. Allen smiled. "You have done your homework. Yes, I contend he would have truly been a great player had he pitched for a stronger ball club."

Some of the other pitchers on that talented staff were much like diamonds in the rough. Each was starting to make his reputation as a tough competitor around the National League in '37. Yet, each was still a season or two away from the banner headlines he would earn.

Bucky Walters and Claude Passeau, for instance, were two other very capable and respected Phillies on that same pitching staff who came up in our discussion. Of course, this was before Walters hit the peak of his career as a prominent pitcher for Cincinnati, while Passeau went on to many productive seasons primarily as a Chicago Cub. These two pitchers would combine for 360 total victories at the end of their careers with the major portion of their successes coming after departing the Philadelphia Phillies.

"What can you tell me about Chuck Klein?" I asked.

"Ah, yes, the great power-hitting outfielder," Allen mused.

"I know he hit 300 career home runs while on his way to induction into the National Baseball Hall of Fame. You guys played your home games in the old Baker Bowl back then, didn't you? And wasn't it referred to as the band box because of the short distances to the outfield walls? And is that why Chuck Klein was able to hit so many homers?"

Allen chuckled. "Well, let me say this. We used to hear that old stadium referred to as the cracker box, but you may be right. Also, right field was the only short fence. The other distances to left and center were pretty normal, but right field was only 280 feet in the corner. Klein, you must remember, did not hit all of his home runs at home in Philadelphia. He hit quite a few on the road at other fields, too. He was a marvelous hitter!"

As I was listening and trying to absorb as much as possible, I could not help but recall how Mrs. Allen had warned me on the phone that her husband's memory was not as good anymore. It was apparent that at least on that day his recollections were sharp, sharp enough, in fact, to not only remember his teammates but to rattle off the distance down the right field line at the home stadium, 65 years later! Mr. Allen seemed to be willing and anxious to continue.

"Doug, I remember at the end of the 1937 season when my manager Jimmy Wilson advised me of his plans to use me as a starting pitcher the following year."

Wilson had been impressed with the velocity of Earl's fastball. However, something dreadfully mysterious happened over the winter of 1937-38, something that would be a devastating, inexplicable nightmare for a young, promising pitcher like Earl Allen.

Over the off-season months, Earl threw no baseballs and only played a little basketball. His plan was to rest up, stay loose, and be ready for another year of baseball by spring. Then, upon his arrival at the Phillies training camp, he found that the speed of his fastballs had vanished. During the past season, Earl estimated that he was throwing in excess of 90 miles per hour.

"Now, I couldn't break a glass window pane," he lamented.

There was no known injury, no pain, and nothing to indicate that something was wrong. He was examined by the Phillies' team doctors and several other physicians along the East Coast. No one seemed to have any answers. He even traveled to West Virginia and bathed in the healing waters of the natural hot springs. Still no improvement.

So what had started, not long before, as a hopeful and promising major league career was no longer a possibility for the "Thin Man." His entire career in the big leagues was closed out after only 12 innings pitched over a span of three ballgames.

"I'm just happy for the time I did have in baseball," he said. "No real regrets."

Mr. Allen signed an index card and a couple of baseballs I had brought. He also gave me a small photo of himself from his minor league days, which he also signed. It was one from a batch of pictures that he had recently had printed from his original. He had these photos on hand so he could be accommodating to collectors who might want one. He showed me several pieces of mail stacked next to his easy chair. Each was a letter requesting his autograph.

"I receive one or two requests a week for autographs," Mr. Allen said incredulously. "We always make sure each gets a prompt reply."

"We even had to add a little return postage on one not too long ago," Mrs. Allen added. "It seems the postal rates increased after this person wrote to us. But that's no problem. We don't mind helping out."

Just as Earl was applying his signature to the last baseball, his eight-year-old granddaughter Emily rushed into the house with one of her neighborhood friends for some of Grandmother's Kool-Aid. With her face flushed from the heat, Emily stopped abruptly when her grandfather handed her a signed baseball to pass to me.

"That's about as good as I can do," he said as he put away his pen.

"What are you all doing?" Emily asked, carefully examining the baseball.

"Granddaddy is signing some autographs for Doug," Mrs. Allen explained.

"But why?" She studied the baseball like a cryptologist scrutinizing a secret code."Wow! This looks like a real autograph," she gasped.

"It sure is, Emily," I said. "That's because your grandfather was a real ballplayer at one time."

"Wow!" she repeated, studying the shaky signature between the seams of the ball.

She gently rotated the ball, admiring the autograph from various angles, like a jeweler marveling at the facets of a newly-cut stone. It was at that moment that she realized her grandfather had been a sports hero, a real baseball player, "Wow," she repeated one more time—her proud smile for her grandfather was his new medal of honor.

"Emily, would you mind taking a picture of your grandparents and me before I leave?"

Emily complied, and I once again felt humbled and honored to be allowed to participate in such a rare and tender family moment.

Mr. Allen gripped my right hand in both of his large hands, stared with intensity directly into my eyes. "You're a fine young man, Doug," he said. "Your visit has been very enjoyable and special for me, too." The eyes of this old gentleman carried a look of deep sincerity and a masculine tenderness that I had previously seen only in my own father. This visit had special meaning for both of us.

"Mr. Allen," I said, "it's like my father used to say, quoting Henry Ford, 'It's always good business when both sides profit,' and I feel as if we have both profited today."

From time to time, I still speak with Mrs. Allen by phone and she tells me that her husband's health is slipping and that he doesn't seem to have the fight to keep going that he used to have. Often I tell her how grateful I am that I was able to spend an hour or two with him at a time when he did feel like having a visitor and sharing with me so freely his memories of the Philadelphia Phillies of 1937.

Thank you, Thin Man. It was a pleasure.

My visit with Mr. and Mrs. Earl Allen in September, 2002; granddaughter, Emily did a great job as our photographer.

CHAPTER 2

Herb Hash—Advice for the Splendid Splinter

"Without the memories of the past, there could be no dreams of greatness in the future; without those passing yesterdays, there can be no bright tomorrows."

- Ford Frick, 1970

The major league baseball season of 1941 is often recalled as the most memorable of all. That summer, fans across the country checked the newspapers daily to see if the Yankee Clipper, Joe DiMaggio, had continued his hitting streak. Joe D. managed to hit safely in an amazing 56 consecutive games that year, an accomplishment that most of us sports know-it-alls feel will never be surpassed. Joe's streak ended on July 17 on a damp, misty night game in Cleveland, thanks in part to some very flashy defensive work by a couple of my beloved Indian heroes: Ken Keltner and Lou Boudreau. This one hitless game for DiMaggio proved to be just a hiccup in what was a white hot batting pace he maintained all season. On July 18, Joe resumed by beginning another string of 33 consecutive games in which he hit safely. These two streaks of 56 and 33 games, which were separated by just one game, resulted in an incredible .357 batting average for Joe at the season's end.

Simultaneously, Ted Williams of the Boston Red Sox was flirting with the coveted .400 batting mark most of the '41 season. On the final day of the schedule, Williams was at an even .400 for the year's average when his manager Joe Cronin offered him the chance to sit out the double header against the Athletics at their home park. Cronin was aware of the pressure weighing on Ted and also the historical impact of his record. But, the confident and arrogant "Splendid Splinter," Ted Williams, was not about to achieve anything the easy way. He played both games that day against Connie Mack's A's and rapped out six base hits in eight at-bats for the afternoon and completed the season with an average of .406! No batter in either the American or National League has reached the .400 level for a season's average in the sixty plus years since.

However, the season of '41 was not a season of peace and comfort for Ted Williams. During that year, not unlike the other years of his career, Ted was at odds with the sport writers and the fans of Boston. This was an ongoing feud that saw few concessions from either side. In one explosive situation early in the year, "The Splinter" seemed to turn everyone except his teammates against him.

At this time, he riled everyone in attendance at Boston's Fenway Park by thumbing his nose and spitting in the direction of spectators who had vented their disapproval of his lack of hustle. The press corps and the fans alike were holding this player in total disdain. Suddenly, Ted realized the hopelessness of it all. He was in a real jam and needed some direction. He had no close family or friends to turn to, except for a select few of his Red Sox teammates who were permitted into his small circle of true personal confidants.

A 33-year-old Boston pitcher named Herb Hash was one such trusted teammate. Herb was approached by Williams in a Boston hotel one day soon after his less than polite gestures had put him at odds with the entire city.

"Herb, I'm in a real mess," Ted confessed. "I don't know which way to turn. Now, you're an educated, reasonable sort of guy with integrity. Do you have any suggestions?"

"Well, I only have advice to give you if you have sincere intentions to follow it," Herb replied.

"Sure, just tell me how to deal with this mess, and I'll give it my best."

"Okay, Ted. Here's what you should do." As if some thought had already been given to the situation, Herb's plan of action came with little hesitation. "We'll be leaving on tomorrow's train to Philadelphia for a three game series. While we're on this road trip, don't say a word to any of the reporters. Now, they will be around you wanting you to talk with them at the railroad station, at our hotel, and at the park. Just ignore them or respond by saying, 'No comment.'"

"Same goes for the trip back," Herb continued. "No conversation with the press. They just want you to give them more fuel for their fire! Now, once we get back to Fenway for our first game back home," Herb added, "you will need to hit that ball out of the park as early in the game as you can and that should help settle things down for you—for a while, anyway."

"Thanks, Herb. It sounds like a smart, logical plan to me," replied a grateful Ted Williams.

And so it happened. The Red Sox enjoyed another successful road trip in the "City of Brotherly Love" while Williams snubbed the press. But their inevitable return to Fenway Park for the first game of a home stand put Ted again in a boiling pot of jeering fans. But as the magic of baseball would have it, he came to the plate in the home half of the first inning with a runner on base and quickly gave Boston a 2-0 advantage by driving a long home run into the right field bleachers! And that's a true story!

Or so it was declared to me by Herb Hash himself, some 62 years later when I visited him in April 2003.

"Yes, indeed. That's just the way it happened. And I tell you, when Ted hit that homer and began to run the bases, the entire crowd came to its feet! By the time he reached third base the whole stadium was yelling and applauding him! Yes, sir, and that's a true story!"

Herbert Howard Hash was born February 13, 1911, in the tiny town of Woolwine, Virginia. Following a celebrated athletic career in high school and later at the University of Richmond, Herb went on to play baseball professionally at the various levels within the Red Sox farm system. He reached the top of the heap in 1940 when he was recalled to the Boston major league roster for the regular season.

"What a team that was!" Herb recalled. "There were some big names on that roster, many who ended up in the Baseball Hall of Fame, and I became friends with all of them! Let's see. There was Jimmie Foxx, Lefty Grove, Ted Williams, Bobby Doerr, and Joe Cronin—all great guys who were eventually elected to the Hall of Fame!"

Herb Hash a Red Sox rookie in 1940

These days, Mr. Hash resides in an elegant retirement facility in Culpeper, Virginia, not far from the place of his birth. A kind and gracious man, now in his 90s, he seems always ready for visitors and conversation. Herb is generous with his views and advice on subjects from baseball to politics to fishing to dining out. He maintains a joyous approach to living each day while at the same time savoring his full, rewarding past, which he loves to share.

My first contact with Mr. Hash took place earlier in 2003. Naturally, I wrote to him to request an autograph. However, in my letter, I also mentioned that I sometimes travel through that portion of the state and wondered if he would mind if I dropped in for a visit.

After only a few days, I received a positive reply. He complied by not only sending several examples of his signature, but also enclosing a short note which read, "Doug, anytime you are out this way, give me a call. I would be happy to meet you. (phone number included). Herb Hash."

I had already planned a trip across the state to visit my sister on her farm in the Virginia mountains, so by telephone, I made arrangements to visit Mr. Hash on the way.

His place was an easy drive on that cold February Sunday through the still sleepy city of Culpeper. Most of the recent snow had melted, and the roads were clear. The frosted rolling hills sparkled under the sun.

His home is situated on stately grounds high on a hill above a winding, paved driveway. The main building is a massive multi-level brick structure with white columns flanking the entrance. The spacious campus and antebellum architecture complemented the landscape.

When I arrived, Herb was relaxing in his one-bedroom apartment, which was neat and decorated with a sportsman's touch. Answering the door with a wide smile, Herb offered a gracious welcome and firm handshake.

"Good to see you. Glad you made it today. Come on in and have a seat." His energetic welcome made it quite clear that he was not just happy to have company, but he was also anxious to talk baseball.

Our conversation began by Herb getting the preliminaries out of the way first. He spoke about how he had been residing at the retirement community for about two years. He explained how life had presented him with a lot of changes in recent years. All of his children were grown with families of their own. But the biggest adjustment of them all was having to deal with the loss of his wife Ruth, who died in 1987. He continued to explain that his current place was not "home." But it was still nice in many ways.

He was pleased with the care and attention he was receiving, and the staff members were all wonderful people who saw to his every need.

The walls and shelves around the sitting area were dotted with evidence of his accomplishments in sports: a silhouette of Herb as a collegiate basketball player, framed photos taken at a recent visit to Fenway, and a gigantic marlin mounted near the doorway.

"You see, Doug, this is surely not what you would refer to as a big place I have here, but it's big enough for me and my things. Most of my things are treasures to me, although they might not be worth anything to someone else. Like those pictures over there, behind you," he explained. "They were all taken a year or two ago when my sons took me up to Boston."

"My boys," he continued, "didn't really give me any choice. They just called me and said, 'Get ready. We're all taking a trip to see the Red Sox play.'"

"They had it all arranged with the ball club. When we arrived at the stadium, we were met by team personnel from the front office along with Johnny Pesky, the former shortstop. They gave us all a big welcome and gave me a few small gifts. A lady with the group told me to be sure to pay close attention to the scoreboard during the middle of the third inning. Then, my two sons and one grandson and I were all escorted to our seats, which were special box seats, down front, behind the Red Sox dugout. We were all enjoying ourselves, watching the game. I forget who Boston was playing, but during the third inning, the announcer called for everyone's attention. 'The Red Sox give a special welcome to former pitcher, Herb Hash, who is seated with his family by the Boston dugout. Mr. Hash, please stand up.'"

"At that moment, they had my name on the electronic screen above the outfield wall with the years I played and my stats. The entire audience applauded. That was the greatest moment I have ever experienced in baseball! Tears welled up as I saw my name out there on that screen, and I tell you. . . I felt very emotional, like I was in a dream. Some of the fans came down to my seat and I signed autographs for them throughout the rest of the game. I'll never forget that night!"

As I soon learned, Mr. Hash had many experiences that he will probably never forget. He instructed me to reach under the edge of his bed, next to where I was seated and slide a cardboard box out from its hiding place. Once I pulled the box into view, I quickly recognized that it was filled with old baseballs, each one covered in writing.

"Now, take a look as some of those balls. You'll see that some of my best moments in the game of baseball are represented in that box."

I picked up one baseball at a time and examined each closely, noting the date and score and, in some instances, a city or stadium inscribed. There was one from June 23, 1940, with additional markings of "Cleveland 2 to 0—complete game." Another was marked "6/15/40 at Chicago 5-2, complete game." In addition, there were several balls bearing dates and information from other games in the major leagues and from minor leagues as well. But there was one ball in that trove of relics that was prized more than the others.

"Doug, you'll see one in there that is from Memorial Day weekend, 1940, at Yankee Stadium. That's when I worked a complete game and beat those damn Yankees in front of a capacity crowd at their own place! That was so satisfying for me because I always hated those Yankees and still do! You know why? I'll tell you. Because they were always so powerful and seemed to beat up on us all the time. I still don't care for them, even today!"

I held the special trophy ball inscribed by Herb: "May 30, 1940, at Yankee Stadium—11-4, complete game."

"Yes, sir," he continued. "New York had such a powerful line-up back then. There were no easy outs on that team, and in that particular game, I was still pitching in the ninth inning and with two outs, the Yankees managed to get two runners on base. I guess I was tiring just a little. That was when our manager, Joe Cronin, who was also the shortstop, called for a time out. He strolled up to me on the mound just as Bill Dickey was about to step up to the plate. He asked if I thought I had enough left to get this final batter out, because Dickey could be a very tough hitter. I told him, 'Sure, I think I can get him.' And that's what happened. I got him to hit a weak little pop-up to shortstop that Cronin himself caught to end the game. Finishing that game by myself sure was a big deal for me. It sure was."

Herb had several other items from his personal collection of baseball keepsakes that he was eager to share. His scrapbook was chocked with newspaper clippings and photos of him with his family. He also had photographs taken of him with Red Sox players and personal letters he had received from some of his famous teammates.

He recalled a morning in a Boston hotel when, as a rookie, Herb walked into a near empty dining room to enjoy a quiet breakfast. Soon after being seated, he recognized one of the greatest of all his fellow Bosox, Jimmie Foxx, having eggs and coffee alone.

Herb politely spoke to the great slugger from his area of the room. "Good morning, Jimmie," he said cautiously, not intending to intrude on the solitude of the muscle-bound sports legend.

Foxx instantly recognized Herb. In a booming, friendly voice, Jimmie startled him, "What's the problem, Rookie? Are you too good to sit with me?"

Herb recalled that first meeting with Jimmie Foxx, the famous "Double X" as a sign of acceptance into major league baseball. For Herb, the friendly gestures of his breakfast partner had christened him as a big leaguer who had finally arrived.

Mr. Hash will tell you that his years in baseball were never anything that he took for granted. He treasured each day, always aware of his blessings, especially each time he buttoned his uniform.

His sense of gratitude is apparent as he continues to highly value each day. "I truly enjoyed who I used to be and I'm happy to be who I am today," he told me during another recent visit to Culpeper.

"Doug, I still get three or four letters each week from people who remember me or know who I am, and they all ask for an autograph. And I'm happy to do it. During the first part of my life, I used to pray that God would give me what I wanted. And you know, He answered and held up His end of the deal. Today, I pray that He will help me give to others what they want."

A golden man, Herbert Howard Hash.

CHAPTER 3

Arthur "Bud" Metheny. . .
That's M-E-T-H-E-N-Y !

"It's a haunted game in which every player is measured against the ghosts of all who have gone before."

--Ken Burns

During World War II, the country was forced to enjoy many of its customs on a smaller scale. Smaller portions of so many commodities were all that was available. That is when the great American spirit showed its real strength. That is also when the Americans of that time—the Greatest Generation—stepped up to the plate, and each person seemed to be willing to make sacrifices and fulfill his or her duties. Sugar, metals, gasoline, coffee, and rubber were all in short supply, and each required a coupon from a ration book that had to be redeemed with payment whenever purchases were made.

Neither was baseball immune to the cutbacks needed for our war effort. Many of the greatest names in American sports were missing from the daily box scores during the seasons of 1942 through 1945. Ted Williams, Joe DiMaggio, Hank Greenberg, and Bob Feller were among those who answered the call to duty by enlisting in the Armed Forces. Baseball continued through World War II, even though the level of talent was not what the American fan was accustomed to.

But baseball was excused. Sure, talent was off. So were salaries for players. So was attendance at the games. However, at the insistence of President Franklin Roosevelt, the game continued. FDR felt that our national pastime would provide a much needed diversion for the men and women who were working long shifts in national defense jobs. Baseball, along with Hollywood filmmakers, offered two of the very few sources of light and relief which continued nonstop during this, one of the darkest periods in world history.

The changes in baseball were often easy to spot. For example, the St. Louis Browns made a rare escape from the depths of the American League standings and won the team's only league championship in 1944. The following season, the Browns included on their roster, an outfielder, who had just one arm. The player, Pete Gray, still managed a batting average of .218! All teams carried members who would otherwise be retired, injured, or in the minor leagues during the four seasons of the war years.

The New York Yankees continued their dominance of the American League at the start of the war. The Yankees, led by manager Joe McCarthy, captured the American League flag in both 1942 and 1943. Each of those years, the Yanks faced the St. Louis Cardinals in the World Series. St. Louis won in '42, taking the series four games to one. New York became world champions in 1943 by returning the favor and beating the Cardinals four games to one.

The 1943 edition of the Yankees included a 28-year-old rookie outfielder who showed considerable promise. This new major leaguer was Arthur Beauregard Metheny, from St. Louis, Missouri. Better known as "Bud," this rookie seemed to be a good fit in the Yankee lineup, which featured several prominent holdovers from the great pre-war Bronx Bombers. Charlie Keller, Bill Dickey, and Joe Gordon were the cornerstones of that club, while Bud Metheny was one of the more impressive newcomers, appearing in more than 100 games during the season. He hit nine home runs and batted a solid .261. Metheny remained with the Yanks for a few years after his rookie year, leaving the team during the 1946 season. The timing of his departure from New York and the big leagues is an indicator of his value as a player. Bud stayed on with the Yankees for a while, even after two great outfielders—Tommy Henrich and Joe DiMaggio—returned from military service. Metheny completed his baseball career with a .247 batting average, a World Series ring, and a lot of great memories.

Bud went on to have a remarkable career in sports for many years following his departure from the Yankees. He became baseball coach, basketball coach, and eventually the Athletic Director at Old Dominion University in Norfolk, Virginia. He was such a successful mainstay at the university that the athletic stadium at the school still bears his name: The Arthur "Bud" Metheny Sports Complex.

I first contacted Mr. Metheny in 1986 by writing to him at his home and asking him for his signature. I also inquired how he managed to settle in Norfolk, Virginia, from St. Louis by way of New York. Furthermore, I asked for his opinion about whom he felt was baseball's best manager, past or present.

Mr. Metheny's response was quick and thorough. He wrote back explaining that he enjoyed living in coastal Virginia, and the area was his wife's preference because she loved the ocean. Thus, the area suited them both. He continued his letter by explaining how Joe McCarthy was, in his opinion, the greatest manager because of his game strategy and his ability to handle the men. He wrote that Joe seemed to know exactly "when to be calm and when to be fiery." Bud was not alone in his esteem for McCarthy who was inducted into the National Baseball Hall of Fame in 1957.

There were a few times during the 1990s that I saw Mr. Metheny at Harbor Park in Norfolk. There the Norfolk Tides, a minor league team, would annually have a special night to honor members of the Tidewater Baseball Shrine. Bud was always invited and regularly attended and participated in the pre-game ceremonies. He and the other members in attendance would be recognized and applauded. And during each of those events, I would make a special effort to go to the Tides' game on Shrine Night, just to see Mr. Metheny as well as other former players and coaches who had a significant impact on baseball in the Tidewater area. All of those old-timers seemed to enjoy the recognition. Pleasant to talk with, they were always generous with their autographs.

In 1998 I arranged a visit to the home of Mr. and Mrs. Metheny. Both were receptive to the idea of my visiting. When I suggested the visit, Bud expressed over the phone how he always enjoyed "talking baseball" as long as he felt well and didn't have other company scheduled to visit.

The Methenys lived in an exclusive retirement community. Each cottage was unique with a modern design and situated on a well-manicured lawn landscaped with crepe myrtles, Japanese holly, and red geraniums. Mrs. Metheny greeted me at the door and welcomed me into the living room where Bud was relaxing in his brown leather recliner. We shook hands and exchanged cordial greetings, and then Bud pointed to the pictures hanging in the hallway. "Since you are such a big baseball fan, Doug, you need to see my pictures."

The hall was replete with framed Yankee photographs as well as awards and pictures from his coaching days at Old Dominion University. His pride was apparent when he directed my attention to the end of the hall.

"Have you seen this picture before?" he asked.

Just like a schoolboy who had studied his lesson, I was fast with the answer. "Yes, sir, I am familiar with that one." I studied the **photograph of Babe Ruth's Farewell Day at Yankee Stadium back in 1948.**

Bud then indicated the row of former Yankees in their pinstriped uniforms lined along the baseline, each observing the famous farewell ceremony. "That's me, there," he beamed and pointed to one of the players in the line. "I was invited to be there that day to honor The Babe."

Mrs. Metheny took pride in her husband's pictures and awards, and during our conversation, she added details about the plaques and pictures. Her participation in the visit and her proud demeanor attested to the fact that Bud's sports career was not a solo flight. Instead, it had been a long, celebrated journey the two shared.

"Are you going to show Doug the ball?" she asked Bud.

"Oh, yes, I sure am," he responded, and he quickly padded down the hall, returning with a baseball housed in a plastic, transparent cube.

"You might enjoy taking a look at this," he said handing me the ball.

I recognized at once the unmistakable signature of Babe Ruth boldly inscribed between the seams on the sweet spot.

"The Babe himself gave me this ball on that day back in '48," he boasted. "What a special, yet sad day, that was for all of us. That was Ruth's last time in a uniform, and he died soon after."

Mr. Metheny's highly prized baseball was quite impressive to me. I told him that I had many nice autographed pieces in my own collection, but nothing could measure up to his baseball in rarity or value. His pride of ownership caught me by surprise. Indeed, even ex-major league players have heroes.

Bud and his wife Francis enjoyed a few more years together before they had to confront various health issues. I never saw Mr. Metheny again after the summer of 1998. I imagine Bud's failing health prevented him from attending games or making appearances after our visit. However, this lovely couple proved to take each step through life together. The ties of their connection ran deep and true.

On the night of January 2, 2003, Francis died at their home following a long fight with cancer. Bud, who was 87, was suffering from diabetes and coronary complications and was in a nursing facility across town. He passed away that same night, less than two hours later. They had wed on Valentine's Day, 1941. After more than 60 years of marriage, they both knew it was no time to start doing things separately.

Before the end of our visit that summer, I asked Bud, "Do you, by any chance, ever get out to attend any of the Old Dominion University baseball games, at the Metheny Sports Complex?"

"Well, Doug, I was recently there when my grandchildren were here for a visit. They had grown restless after a few days into their stay here and were in need of some fresh air and outdoor activity. For the first time in a long time, we went out to see the college team play.

"As we approached the ticket booth, the young coed working the window asked, 'How many tickets?'"

"No tickets," I answered. "I don't think we will need any. We should be on your pass list."

" 'Okay, sir, let me check the list,' she said."

"That's when the young lady grabbed the handy clipboard with the affixed pass list and inquired, 'What is the name, sir?'"

" 'Metheny,'" I replied."

"The student scanned the list, starting at the top and moving her finger along the page. 'Metheny,' she mumbled. 'Metheny, Metheny,' she repeated. 'I can't seem to find you, sir. Let me try again.'"

"Again she scanned the list. 'I still can't find your name,' she said with concern. 'How do you spell that?'"

" 'M-E-T-H-E-N-Y,' I spelled patiently, deliberately, and calmly."

" 'M-E-T-H-E-N-Y,' she repeated."

"Again she asked me how to spell my name, and again I said, 'M-E-T-H-E-N-Y. Metheny, just like it reads on that archway there, over the entrance gate.' And I pointed."

   " 'Okay,' she said and again scrutinized the list on the clipboard as she softly repeated the name to herself again and again. Suddenly, her eyes widened in realization, 'Oh, my. Metheny! Oh, I am very sorry. Yes, Mr. Metheny! You folks go right on in. And I hope you enjoy the game!'"

As a young promising Yankee outfielder- Bud Metheny

CHAPTER 4

"Deacon" Murray

"Baseball can be as simple as a bat and ball or as complex as the American spirit it symbolizes."

-Ernie Harwell

A big surprise awaited our country, especially the political pollsters, when presidential results were made official in 1948. Harry Truman had been elected the 33rd President of the United States. That same year, movie-goers were watching Humphrey Bogart and Lauren Bacall in *Key Largo*, while Art Mooney topped pop music surveys with his hit "I'm Looking Over a Four-Leaf Clover." Our nation mourned the death of the greatest sports figure of them all when Babe Ruth died at age 53 in August.

That was also the last year the Cleveland Indians would lay claim to the title "World Champions." The World Series of '48 came to within one game of being an all-Boston confrontation as the Indians and Red Sox finished the season tied for first place in the American League. A single playoff game was played in Boston's Fenway Park to break that deadlock. In that winner-take-all contest, Cleveland player-manager, Lou Boudreau socked two home runs to propel the Tribe to an 8-3 win past the Red Sox and on to the World Series to face Boston's other major league club, the National League Champion Boston Braves. The Indians kept their momentum alive and defeated the Braves four games to two. It was Cleveland's only World Championship, except for 1920. There has been none since.

The Indians of '48 briefly carried a 30-year-old journeyman catcher on their roster. This veteran of the minor leagues from Spring Hope, North Carolina, was Raymond Lee Murray, who made his debut in the major leagues by taking the field for just four games that season for Cleveland. Never becoming a star player or even an everyday catcher, Ray found ways to maintain regular employment in the big leagues from the season of '48 through '54 with Cleveland and also the Athletics and Orioles. Among the few notable highlights of his career is his inclusion, albeit a minor role, on the 1948 Champion Indians. Also, in his final year as an active player, he was a member of the Orioles during their inaugural season in Baltimore.

Baseball lore has it that Ray picked up the nickname "Deacon" early in his career. It is told that while in the minor leagues, he often "preached" to his teammates on bus trips and sometimes in the clubhouse. Who knows how far Ray carried his preaching tendencies? Maybe he only mentioned his beliefs to others when the topic came up during idle times. Perhaps he was on a daily crusade to share his faith. Either way, the tag "Deacon" is one that brings with it some degree of integrity as opposed to other baseball names like Stinky, Muddy, Stump, or Worm.

He was a big man physically at 6 feet 3 inches and over 200 lbs. Most likely he was slow afoot like most catchers. Maybe Ray was a little too slow for his own good. He played 250 games in his major league career and is credited with just one stolen base! That's right, just one!

However, his tardiness on the base paths was in no way reflected in his promptness for answering his mail. It was not until December 2, 2002, that I finally wrote to Mr. Murray. That is quite late for me to be getting in touch with him to request an autograph, considering he was an Indian player for parts of several seasons. I wrote to him at his home in Fort Worth, Texas, and included in my request, was a 1954 baseball card that pictured him as a member of the Philadelphia Athletics, along with the usual blank index card, hoping he would sign each of them.

His response was in my mailbox in just four days! On December 6, I received both items autographed as requested. I had never had such a quick, timely reply in all the years I had been collecting signatures by mail. Quite a surprise!

But there was something extra included in my return mail. I noticed the letter I had written to Mr. Murray had been sent back along with the signed cards. Added to the bottom of my letter was a poignant inscription:

"Doug—I lost my wife, Jacque,
 October 28, 2002."

Just two lines written to me, an admirer but a stranger, nonetheless. It served an unmistakable indication of his grief and personal pain.

In sympathy, I responded right away. In my letter, I thanked him for taking the time to sign for me and that truly I appreciated his prompt reply. I went on the express my condolences for his loss and added that I would keep him in my prayers, asking God to supply him with the comfort, strength, and peace he would need. I sensed that the holiday season was the time he would require extra helpings of each.

I believe Ray received that comfort and peace. The Deacon passed away three months later at the age of 85.

Now, if I thumb through my collection of autographed gum cards, I can pick out the 1954 Topps, No. 49, Ray Murray. The back of this card has the usual biographical information, including height, weight, last season's stats, and hometown. But, there is also a brief illustrated story that tells us a bit more about Ray. It seems that one day, while working behind the plate, Ray was having continual differences of opinion with the home plate umpire. The ump's ideas of balls and strikes were obviously different from Ray's. Instead of getting loud with the "man in blue" and having an argument, Ray reached into his pocket and then quietly handed the umpire a business card from the local eye doctor. Ray then discreetly suggested that the umpire call to schedule himself for an appointment. No aggression. No anger. Just a subtle suggestion from the "Deacon."

"Deacon" Ray Murray-1954

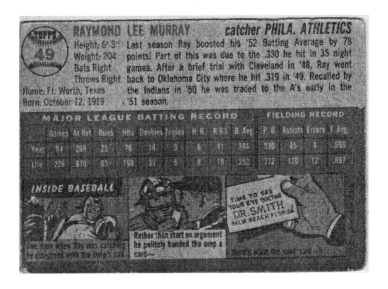

Ray Murray suggested that the umpire make an appointment to get his vision checked.

CHAPTER 5

"Dot" and "Buck" Marrow—It's All Ancient History

"Wisdom is the principal thing; therefore, get wisdom and with all thy getting, get understanding."

- Proverbs 4:7

Part I

It is often said there is much to be learned while seated at the feet of the elderly, and many never take advantage of such an opportunity. Those of us who do are often pretty far along in years when we realize what we might have missed by not paying attention to those who are wiser.

The term "generation gap" was one that was used often during my youth in the '60s. No one, it seemed to me, was more conscious of such a gap than I was when I was 16 years old. Then suddenly at 25, the gap began to close. There were those from previous generations that I not only appreciated more than ever, but there were also those whose advice and direction I sought. Now, at 52 I find the gap is miniscule.

This next account is about an exceptional person at whose feet I have spent many hours. By the latter part of 1996, I was very confident regarding my knowledge of local former baseball players. I was sure I was aware of all ex-big leaguers, living or deceased, whether I had tried to contact them or not. However, one name on my address list belied my confidence: Charles K. "Buck" Marrow" at 203 River Road, Newport News, Virginia. Buck Marrow, I thought, had passed away years ago. Could I be wrong? I vaguely recalled having researched his 1930s pitching career.

Right away I consulted a Newport News phone book and found a listing. Next, I studied the Baseball Encyclopedia and verified his teams and playing seasons. It stated that Marrow had played for Detroit in 1932 and Brooklyn from 1937 to 1938. There was also a death date listed as November 21, 1982. However, the address listed was more recent than the Baseball Encyclopedia, so I dialed the number in the phone book, wishing that my address list was correct, and a pleasant, elderly, feminine voice answered.

"Is this the Marrow residence?" I asked.

"Yes, it is," she replied.

"May I speak to Mr. Marrow," I said tentatively.

"I'm sorry," she answered, "but he is deceased. He passed away in 1982."

"I am so sorry," I apologized. "I did not know, and I did not mean to disturb you. Is this Mrs. Marrow?"

"It is," she said cheerfully." And that's perfectly all right. You did not disturb me. Is there anything I can help you with?"

Embarrassed, I stumbled over my words. "You see, Mrs. Marrow, I am what you would call a baseball nut, and I was hoping to meet your husband and get his autograph."

She must have sensed a true tone of apology, because she quickly came to my aid. "I am sure if Buck were alive he would have been more than glad to meet you and would have accommodated you in any way he could." She continued, "Buck was one who just loved people, and he enjoyed it when someone asked for an autograph. But if you were to give me your name and address, maybe I could help you out."

Before hanging up, I thanked her and again apologized for having bothered her, but Mrs. Marrow continued to reassure me that my call was not an intrusion.

And then I waited, puzzled by what to expect.

One week later, I received an envelope. Inside was a postcard-sized black and white photograph of Buck Marrow wearing a Brooklyn Dodger uniform, most likely a print, but obviously a picture from the late 1930s. On the reverse side was an ink signature that had been cut from an old cancelled check and taped neatly near the bottom edge: C.K. Marrow.

A short note included in the envelope said, "Dear Douglas, I hope this will help fill the void in your autograph collection. Sincerely, Dorothy Marrow."

All of this from a lady who didn't know me from Adam!

Recognizing the time and effort it took Mrs. Marrow to send the picture, I immediately phoned her to express my gratitude.

"I know Buck would want me to do such things on his behalf," she said graciously.

While we chatted, I asked Mrs. Marrow if she ever saw or heard from any of Buck's old teammates. She indicated that it had been ages since she had talked with anyone, and she had probably forgotten a lot of their names. However, she did mention that Babe Ruth had been a coach for the Dodgers back when Buck was on the team, and that the famous KiKi Cuyler had been one of his minor league managers back then.

She told me that one of Buck's favorite tales was from the early years when he was with Detroit. She said as a Tiger pitcher, he faced Babe Ruth when he came to bat in an exhibition game. "You'll have to pardon my language, but Buck said, 'when Babe came to bat against me, I hit him right in the butt!' That's just what he said."

I told her how I enjoyed talking with her and how I enjoyed hearing about Buck. "Don't be surprised," I said, "if I call back sometime and want to talk baseball again."

Welcoming the idea, she said, "Call me anytime, Doug. I'll be glad to tell you about anything I can remember, which may not be very much because so much of it was a long time ago! It's all ancient history now."

I took her up on that invitation and found she had a considerable repertoire of old stories about the Dodgers of 1937 and 1938. She was able to recall not only the players' names but the names of their wives as well. She spoke of how she and Buck came from rural areas of North Carolina and how she especially had a lot to learn and adjust to when the two of them rented an apartment and lived in the big city of Brooklyn. She shared openly with me her memories of 60 years ago, and although she enjoyed talking about those days, she couldn't have enjoyed it as much as I did listening to her. It was during one of these early phone calls that she insisted that I not refer to her as Mrs. Morrow.

"Just call me Dot. That's what all of my friends call me, and you are certainly a friend."

With that, a delightful relationship was born.

Dot told me of a huge scrapbook she had assembled long ago dedicated solely to the subject of Buck's baseball years. "That scrapbook is around here somewhere. I still have it and if you would like, you may come by the house and take a look at it."

At first, I was really surprised by her kind invitation. After all, we had never met other than the telephone conversations, but need I say how quickly I took her up on her offer? I made the 25-mile drive over to the Hilton neighborhood of Newport News.

Her neighborhood was quiet and nostalgic with its tree-lined streets and larger older homes situated near the banks of the James River. The charming neighborhood is lined with sidewalks and dotted with 500 two-story homes built just after World War I as part of the Federal War Housing project. In addition, there are several churches, an elementary school, and rows of specialty shops. The entire village is bisected by Main Street.

Dot's house on River Road was one that blended in with the other large old homes and in front was her blue Ford Tempo with a Duke University decal in the back window. I rang the doorbell and was greeted by a small, thin, gray-haired lady with a warm, welcoming smile.

"Come right in, Doug," she said enthusiastically. "It's so nice to meet you."

We settled in the living room. "Here is the old scrapbook," she said, pointing to the bulging volume lying on the coffee table. "I think you'll enjoy it. Can I get you some coffee or tea?"

The scrapbook was stuffed with pictures of Buck. Some were of his minor league years with the Toronto Maple Leafs, others from his time as a pitcher with the Minneapolis Millers. Still others were of old newspaper clippings, now yellow with age, and old snapshots. Some photos featured ball players that Dot could not identify. "This is all ancient history," she said.

There were several pictures of Buck with the Dodgers. "Those years in Brooklyn were the ones we enjoyed the most. We met so many wonderful people there."

Backtracking, she added, "Well, not just there in Brooklyn. We met nice people everywhere we went in baseball. But we sometimes encountered some rude people, too. Those Dodger fans in New York would come out to the games, and they could be really rude and say some ugly things at times. Sometimes they would direct their nasty comments to the players' wives. That's the reason I asked the team office to allow me to exchange my ticket in the box seats that were for family members only for regular seats. That way, people in the crowd would not know I was a player's wife. It was not that I didn't like the other Dodger wives, because I did enjoy most of them. But it was nice to get away from the harassment, especially if it was your husband who was having a bad game. The other wives were in for a bad time when the team was losing. The players' wives were a great bunch of girls for the most part. I say 'girls' because that's what we were back then, just young girls," she said wistfully.

"A few of the wives were a little snobby," Dot continued. "They thought they were 'somebody' just because their husbands were so and so, and they would think that made them a little better than the rest of us. But those were wonderful times. Me being just a country girl from North Carolina, I had a hard time understanding the New Yorkers' accent at times. I didn't even know what some of the people at the ballpark were yelling at the players. It sounded like 'YABUMYA!' It turns out they were saying, 'You bum, you!'"

We didn't just talk baseball that day. Upon inquiring about her daughter Louise and son-in-law Gil, who lived a few miles away with their two daughters Natalie and Kennon, I learned she was quick to add that she was a family-oriented person, and her visits from family members were the best times for her. She invited me to take her scrapbook and make copies of anything inside that I would want. "Just be sure I get it all back," she said. "This is something that will stay in the family. I know it's falling apart, but it has some significance to some of the grandchildren or nephews I'm sure."

During that time, I also shared with her some photos from my collection, pictures that were taken inside my house of racks full of bats, rows of hanging uniforms, and walls covered with framed pictures and plaques, all having to do with baseball. One look at those photos, and Dot remarked, "You *are* a baseball nut, just like you said on the phone!"

Our mutual admiration society led to still more phone calls and more visits. We would occasionally have lunch together at one of her favorite spots near her home: Monty's Penguin, an ice cream and burger place that featured barbecue, which Dot highly recommended. Turns out, she knew what she was talking about. At other times, our getting together was centered around dinner. Dot would insist on treating me to a meal at the country club where she and Buck had been members for many years. And when it would be my turn to pick up the tab, we would do Italian.

Whenever we ran into her friends or neighbors, she was quick to introduce me by saying, "This is Doug Williams from over in Gloucester. He is one of my new friends because when you get to be my age, you'll find you have outlived all of your old ones."

Charles K. Marrow was a pitcher for the
Brooklyn Dodgers in 1937 and 1938.

Part II

The times Dot and I spent together often got away from the subject of baseball, but Buck's name would pop up frequently. After all, the two were married for nearly 50 years, and he wasn't always a baseball player. During World War II, Buck worked in the shipyard in Newport News. At one time, he owned and operated Marrow's Tire Company for years with Dot serving as his bookkeeper. He was also a Sunday school teacher for teenage boys, and he was an elected member of the Newport News City Council. The Marrows reared their daughter Louise, and then lent a hand in bringing up the two granddaughters, as grandparents do. The life Buck and Dot shared was full and rich.

Life for Dot continued at a frenetic pace. She was still driving in town, playing bridge, baking pecan pies, and growing aloe plants. Her love of sports did not wane either. Because Duke University was her alma mater, she followed Blue Devil basketball. She also enjoyed watching pro golf. Consequently, it was no surprise that she readily accepted my invitation to see my "baseball museum."

Upon her arrival at my house, Dot amazed me with her observations. For example, she noted that the double knit material of the newer uniforms was a lot different from the fabric of the old ones she recalled. Also, there was a huge quantity of autographed pictures, which were a mixture of color prints as well as black and whites.

Reflecting, she asked, "The color pictures are mostly modern ball players, aren't they? Because I don't recall there being any like those in Buck's time. That just goes to show how long ago it really was."

One of her comments was most striking. As she pointed to one of the many signed baseballs that are on display, recognizing a familiar name, she remarked, "This ball is signed by Burleigh Grimes, isn't it?"

"It sure is," I answered. "Do you know who he is?"

"I sure do!" she replied. "Isn't he dead?"

"Yes, ma'am," I said, "he died quite a few years ago."

"I thought so," she acknowledged. "Yes, I knew him very well. He was Buck's manager when we were with Brooklyn. He was a nice man, and his wife was just lovely. Buck and I lived with the Grimes for a short while. They invited us to stay with them until we could find our own apartment, and they really took care of us."

An uncanny feeling came over me. Here was someone visiting me and seeing the collection—someone who not only enjoyed baseball of long ago, but who had lived it! Sure she knew who Burleigh Grimes was. This lady was full of surprises.

Another day when I was at her house, Dot piped up, "You know, I have been meaning to mention to you, but I never can think of it when I am with you. I used to go to school at Duke with a boy who went on to play baseball. You might not know of him, but he and I were really good friends at Duke. His name is Bill Werber."

I just about fell off the sofa. "Bill Werber! This is unreal, Dot!" I exclaimed. "Of course, I have heard of him. I just wrote to him about a month or two back to get his autograph and to ask how I could get a copy of his book. And you are friends with him," I said in awe.

"Yes, we were good friends and I'm happy to hear that he is still around because I have not seen or heard from him since our class reunion years ago. It was our 50th, so it must have been back in 1980 that I last saw him. And you know what? He had finished his book at that time, and he gave me a copy of it at the reunion. You can borrow my copy if you want."

It is just incredible how the threads of our lives, generations apart, were woven together into the same intricate canvas. "I would love to borrow your book," I said.

It was not until the fall of 2000 that I found out firsthand just what good friends Dot and Mr. Weber really were. I attended a function in the Philadelphia area, which was a two-day gathering sponsored by the Philadelphia Athletics Historical Society. This was an opportunity for members of the society to meet with several of the former players from this old ball team. Keep in mind that the Athletics team, which is now the Oakland A's, played their last game n Philadelphia in 1954 with the franchise spending several seasons in Kansas City in between. As one can imagine, these ex-athletes were all advancing in years. The ex-Philadelphia player I was most excited about seeing was Bill Werber, 92, who was scheduled to attend.

Soon after my arrival at the convention center, I learned that Mr. Werber was the featured guest that so many had come to see with the hopes of meeting him in person. What a special event this turned out to be.

Mr. Werber, who had played with the Boston Red Sox and the Cincinnati Reds, had started out in the majors as a teammate of Babe Ruth's as a New York Yankee. In addition, he had been the American League leader in stolen bases for 1934, 1935, and then again in 1937.

The keynote speaker at the society's Sunday morning breakfast meeting, which drew several hundred club members and guests, Werber was the hit of the weekend. He was an outstanding speaker, regaling everyone with his recollections of such teammates as Babe Ruth, Lefty Grove, and Jimmie Foxx. I was spellbound. While time had dampened his ability to get around, requiring him to depend on an aluminum walker and some family members, it had not affected his memory or his sense of humor. I was mesmerized, all the while pushing away the irony that diabetes and a double amputation had stolen the legs that had stolen enough bases to make him a three-time stolen base champion in his glory days.

Soon after the breakfast and short intermission, lines were formed by almost everyone in attendance to wait their turns for autographs from the old baseball players. Of course, I was in the longest line, waiting to meet Bill Werber. When my turn finally came, I spoke to him with my usual greeting, "It is a pleasure to meet you, sir." Then I added, "It seems that you and I have a mutual friend, an old classmate of yours from back at Duke."

"Oh, really?" he asked. "And who might that be?"

"Her name is Dot Marrow, but you knew her as Dot Jennette."

"Oh my goodness! You know Dot? How is that girl? Is she okay?"

A priority matter for Bill had now switched from the lengthy line waiting to get to him to the subject of Dot Jeannette Marrow. Nothing else seemed important to him at that moment. Suddenly, he was the one asking the questions, "Where is she living? Can she still dance? How can I get in touch with her?" His eyes gleamed with enthusiasm.

I then explained, "I told Dot that I expected to meet you this weekend and so she said for me to tell you she sends her love and best regards. She also told me to use her maiden name, Jeannette, because you would be more familiar with it."

Mr. Werber was grateful for my passing along Dot's sentiments and also for my having written her phone number and address on a piece of note paper in advance. "She would love to hear from you, Mr. Werber. Please contact her."

"Sure. Tell her I'll do it soon. Now, let me ask a favor of you. Ask Dot if she remembers the day in English class at Duke when I had sneezing powder on the back of my hand. The window was open and a gust of wind came inside and blew that stuff all over! Students all around were sneezing like crazy, and the teacher, Dr. Greene, didn't appreciate it at all! Matter of fact, he gave us all a lecture about how anybody who did something like that was very childish and did not come here to learn. But he said that he didn't know who was responsible and didn't want to know. As best as I can recall, Dot was the only one who knew where the powder came from. She gave me the shame-on-you sign while the teacher was scolding us, but she never told on me. Ask her if she remembers that one and tell her I'm happy to hear from her and that I'll be in touch soon."

Shortly afterward, Dot did receive a letter from Bill, and he also wrote to me, expressing his appreciation for helping him reconnect with his old classmate and friend.

Dot has since moved into an assisted living facility and uses her cane more now, even though she continues to walk a mile each day around the property. She still loves salads, crab cakes, wine, and good conversation. She says she loves it when I come to visit. At 95, she remains a charming and gracious woman, ready to offer her hospitality. Her diminishing eyesight is her biggest obstacle these days. Yet, her dimming vision has not eclipsed her outlook.

As she recently explained, "I am not about to sit here and complain about how bad I've got it. This is not my house, but I can't live alone, so this is the next best thing. I have had a wonderful life. I had a wonderful childhood and a wonderful marriage. I enjoyed being Buck's wife, and I enjoy being a mother and a grandmother. I've had all I could have ever wanted. I might be into my last steps now, but I wouldn't have any business sitting here being depressed or feeling sorry for myself because I have no regrets and I've had it so good for so long."

It has been an honor and privilege to have Dot Marrow as one of my dearest friends. I have learned much from her, and her cheerful and congenial nature as well as her enduring wisdom have added depth and richness to my own life.

Which reminds me. . . .A few years ago I made an earnest attempt to have Buck Marrow enshrined into the Sports Shrine for the Lower Virginia Peninsula. It is incomprehensible that he was omitted. This shrine is a means of honoring our local athletes and those from surrounding cities. I felt Buck was deserving of the honor, especially considering his contribution to the community, not to mention the fact that he won 17 games as a pitcher for the Toronto Maple Leafs in 1933. But after filling out all the necessary applications, making numerous phone calls, and writing countless letters, I received word that Buck Marrow had not been selected.

Incredulous, I immediately telephone Dot. "I just can't believe it, Dot!" I said angrily. "This is just not right! How could they do this? Who around here has a more impressive list of accomplishments than Buck Marrow?"

Dot waited for me to finish my tirade, and then with cool dignity replied, "Doug, calm down. It's okay. We'll be all right. We just need to try another time. Right now, what we need to do is find a way to be happy for the ones who did make it."

In retrospect, my meeting with Dot Marrow was no coincidence. Some things were just meant to be. I treasure our friendship and look forward to the next bit of wisdom she shares with me.

Douglas Williams

Time well spent with my friend Dot Marrow

CHAPTER 6

One Letter Off—Tony Malinosky

"Baseball is a game to be savored rather than taken in gulps."
- Bill Veeck

The Brooklyn Dodgers of 1937 were a hapless bunch. Their ineptness on the diamond resulted in their finishing in sixth place in the then eight-team National League. The fact that the year's final standings left them at 33 ½ games out of first place has never dampened my personal affection for the team. The allure for this particular edition of the "Bums" has everything to do with my precious friendship with Dorothy Marrow. Maybe I am an opportunist to some extent. But I did mention my relationship with Dot in letters I wrote to some of the few surviving teammates of her late husband Buck. This bit of name-dropping sparked some memories and generated some great responses from several former Dodgers of the late thirties who remembered the Marrows.

Ernie Koy, Peter Coscarart, Tot Pressnell, and George Cisar all wrote back and expressed fond recollections. In addition, they asked that I forward their regards to Dot. However, none of them seemed to be as eager to recall their old Dodger days as former infielder Tony Malinosky.

Tony, a native of Collinsville, Illinois, was 27 when he finally made his way to the Brooklyn club of '37, after toiling in the minor leagues for several years. Without a doubt, he thought he had stepped foot into the land of opportunity when he first walked into the Dodgers' clubhouse. This team was quite deserving of their nickname "Dem Bums" as they were affectionately called by the hometown fans. Their roster seemed to be fully stocked with mediocrity. There was just a handful of players who could be classified as competent big leaguers along with more than their share of rookies and sophomores.

The 1937 Dodgers also featured a couple of the true, great players of the game. For example, there was the former batting champion from the 1926 Detroit Tigers, Heinie Manush and Waite Hoyt, pitching star, formerly of the great Yankees team of the 1920s. Both of these future members of the Hall of Fame were getting on in age and well past their prime as athletes, even though Manush flashed one last glimpse of his former greatness in 1937 by finishing the season with a batting average above .330.

Tony came to the club hopeful of nailing down the job as the everyday third baseman. After all, there were several on the team who had arrived on the scene ahead of him. But no one in particular had performed well enough to lay claim to the hot-corner position. Yet, he had no way of knowing that he was destined to be added to the ranks of the disappointed, because 1937 turned out to be Tony's only year in the major leagues. His career was complete after just 79 trips to the plate and a .228 average.

Still, those few short months during the summer of '37 proved adequate time for Tony to make many lasting memories and develop special friendships—some of which were detailed in a 2001 letter I received from Mr. Malinosky, who shared just how deeply he had been impacted by friends made long ago, even if some minor details had faded some over the years.

He wrote that he was delighted to hear from me, especially since I was a friend of Dorothy's. He explained how he and his wife Viola were close friends with the Marrows long ago, so he was saddened to hear from me that Buck had passed away. He himself was still grieving from the recent loss of Viola, who had died in 1999. He also wrote that he and Viola had been friends with Buck and Dot, dating back to the men's time in the minor leagues, when they played together in Louisville along with fellow teammate Dick Bass. He asked that I pass along his best wishes to Dot, saying that he always remembered her as a "great gal."

A couple of days passed before I got the chance to drive over to Dot's residence at a retirement community in nearby Newport News. I couldn't wait long because I was eager to share with her the letter from Mr. Malinosky. After all, the letter was written with her in mind, so my satisfaction was a result of completing the connection between two old friends.

As always, Dorothy greeted me with genuine grace. "Doug, I'm so glad to see you!" she said, hugging me. "Come on in and have a seat. Let me turn some more lights on. Would you like something to drink?" she added, making me feel at home.

"No, thanks, Dot. I'll just have a seat. I don't have but a few minutes, but I do have a letter here that I want to share with you. I just received it a day or two ago, and it's from a man in Oxnard, California, who claims to remember you from many years ago. His name is Tony Malinosky."

"Oh, my! Yes, Tony from baseball!" Dot exclaimed. "I remember Tony very well. Tony and his wife Vi. Her name was really Viola, but we all just called her Vi. They were really nice people. How are they doing?"

"Well Dot, he seems to be doing okay. He wrote about what good friends you all were and how close you were as couples. But Viola died a couple of years ago. It seems that since you were last together he was in World War II and was fortunate to have survived the Battle of the Bulge. Since that time, he has been living in California and spending a lot of his time fishing." I added.

Dot listened intently as I continued, "He writes here, Dot, that he recalls a little dog you and Buck used to have in your apartment. He remembers how fond the two of you were of that dog, and he seems to think the little dog's name was Tippy."

"Oh, my goodness!" Dot said in surprise. "That's amazing. This is like hearing a voice from the past. It really is a voice from my past! But you know what? He's not quite correct. That little dog was Buck's, and he thought so much of that dog. But his name was Nippy, not Tippy. But that's okay. Tony is just one letter off, and that's okay because it's got to have been 60 or 70 years since all of that! Now, if you will, write back to Tony for me and let him know he missed Nippy's name by one letter," she said laughing.

That I did. I've written to Tony a few times since then, on Dot's behalf, and I have also made a few phone calls to his home in California. Communications are somewhat restricted when it comes to this rediscovered friendship. When I call Tony, I must settle for leaving a message on his answering machine because his hearing requires him to play the recording repeatedly until he gets the full message. Then he will respond to my call by mail. On the other hand, I will answer in writing for Dot, whose poor vision prevents her from reading or writing for herself.

   With a little help, however, this renewed friendship continues. The contacts are infrequent but at least each is aware that the other is still out there somewhere and still remembers. Tony feels like I should board a plane with Dot and fly out to sunny, warm California to visit. For now, though, there still remain some remnants of the '37 Dodgers that are connected.

Tony Malinosky-Brooklyn Dodgers, 1937—
his only season in the major leagues

CHAPTER 7

A Catcher's Mitt and Forty Years

"Playing baseball is not real life. It's a fantasy world. . . It's a dream come true."

- Dale Murphy

Looking back at the decade of the 1960s, we see a time of drastic change for our country. Historically, the period rivals any other when it comes to social and cultural divisions, new ideas about religion, and political upheaval. As the decade began, our nation took its first steps in the direction of racial equality and civil rights. American life seemed to transform from one of settled comfort and conformity to a life of uncertainty and fear.

In 1962, "The Long Distance Call" aired on *Leave It to Beaver*, the episode when Beaver and his friends called Dodger pitcher Don Drysdale, who played a cameo role.

In addition, UFO sightings and reports flourished. Were these alien visitors friends or foes? Our own manned space capsules were now, not just traveling upward, but were orbiting our planet, as astronaut John Glenn did on February 20, 1962, in the Mercury capsule *Friendship 7.* Were we venturing to regions that we had no business exploring? And the dreaded Soviet Union had missiles with nuclear warheads positioned in Cuba, aimed directly at our mainland. Were we facing total annihilation in October 1962 if our enemy made good on its threat?

The popular hit movie *American Graffiti* gave us a fairly accurate account of some of the fun things that were happening in 1962. That story featured hot rods, drive-ins, and great rock'n roll, delivered on A.M. radio by the legendary "Wolfman Jack." In addition, there were three-speed English racer bicycles, backyard bomb shelters, and a new oral vaccine for polio. The year 1962 was also when a certain family loaded up the truck and moved to Beverly. . .Hills, that is. Things were going well for the Clampetts in that season.

Things were going well for the New York Yankees in that season, too. Their newest star player, Tom Tresh, was selected American League Rookie of the Year, while their brightest star, Mickey Mantle was named the League's Most Valuable Player. They were also world champions again after defeating Willie Mays and the San Francisco Giants in the World Series, four games to three.

As a fourth grader that year, I had few pressing responsibilities. For the most part, all I had to keep up with was feeding my dog, mowing the grass, and doing enough homework to maintain A's and B's.

The stories on the evening news with Chet Huntley and David Brinkley neither affected me nor concerned me. The big deal for me personally was that I would be turning ten years old on November 10th.

At this point, my passion for the game of baseball had not just sprouted but was well on its way to blossoming. I had already accumulated a nice collection of bubblegum cards. This precious box of pasteboards included a good assortment of football cards, but the majority of them were baseball, and they were my favorites.

In particular, it was the baseball cards of catchers that seemed to intrigue me most. Maybe it was the catchers' gear that captivated me. Or maybe it was the way they appeared in the "in-action" shots with their baseball caps on backwards with brims snapped up, along with the suspender-like straps of the chest protector obscuring the uniform numbers. Whatever the case, there was something about that "ready for battle" look of the catchers that fascinated me. That fascination was so strong, so consuming, that I felt like I had no choice but be a "backstop" myself.

I asked my parents for nothing else but a catcher's glove for my birthday. If I could get at least that catcher's mitt, then I could start emulating the crouched posture of Del Rice on his 1958 card (Number 51) or Ed Sadowski on his 1962 card (Number 569).

So, it was a couple of weeks before my big day that I submitted my catcher's mitt birthday request to my dad, who offered no overt opposition. Instead, he simply replied, "We'll just have to see, son."

One day when we were playing catch, though, Dad looked at my scrunched position and said, "You know, you'll probably need a catcher's mask, too, if you're going to squat down every time I throw you the ball."

I was hopeful.

Finally, the big day arrived, and it was to be one of the most anticipated birthdays I would ever know. That morning I opened the Rawlings Sports Co. boxes with the fervent readiness of a rookie ready to sign with a big league team. Inside I found a mitt and a mask. A mitt *and* a mask! It was hard to contain my joy.

The mitt had an extra feature: the manufacturer's label of "Hank Foiles, Professional Model." Didn't I have a 1961 Hank Foiles' card? Number 277? Foiles, I recalled, was from Norfolk, Virginia, just a short drive from our home. And from then on, this luminous moment was anchored to my personal joy whenever I saw the block letters of Foiles' name emblazoned in the leather of my very own Rawlings catcher's mitt.

"Mom! Dad! Thank you. This is the best birthday ever!" And it remains one of my happiest days—the kind of day Emily in Thornton Wilder's *Our Town* would have chosen to relive.

Hank Foiles' 1961 baseball card, cards
of catchers were my favorites.

I never did develop into the catcher that I dreamed of becoming, nor even the caliber of catcher I imitated while wearing the mitt and mask. Shortly thereafter, however, while playing Little League Baseball, I proved to be a more than adequate contact hitter and dependable outfielder. Never once, though, did I ever squat behind the dish to try myself as a catcher, either in a game or even in practice.

Since grade school, Little League, and feeding my dog, the years have passed "like so many summer fields" as the Jackson Browne song goes. There was high school. In addition, I had to deal with work and mortgages and divorces—the paperwork of adults, and the details of life. There were moments when I exhibited flashes of conformity and the semblance of settling into adulthood. While an affable, responsible man, I take pride in my spontaneity and my ability to embrace life with boldness.

By 1996, I had built an impressive collection of baseball memorabilia. Some might call it a "magnificent obsession." Through sports collectors' shows and by mail, I had acquired the signatures of many famous former players. One of the most treasured items in the collection is a baseball autographed by members of the 1955 Cleveland Indians. This ball now is covered with the signatures of sixteen members of that team, including all the stars and Hall of Fame players, including Bob Lemon, Early Wynn, Herb Score, Larry Doby, and , of course, Bob Feller. Many of the lesser known members of the '55 Tribe are also included. Obtaining those names on the ball required some travel, some letter writing, some cold calling by phone, and some help from collectors in other states.

Now, Hank Foiles had been a prominent player in the major leagues for many seasons. He is probably best remembered as a Pittsburgh Pirate, which was the team he represented in 1957 when he was selected as a catcher for the National League All-Star team. He also played with the Baltimore Orioles, Cincinnati Reds, and the Los Angeles Angels. And as I later learned through poring over the Baseball Encyclopedia, he had been a member of the '55 Indians.

By the 1990s, Mr. Foiles was in his mid-sixties and well known in the Norfolk, Virginia, area as a successful businessman. It seemed to be an opportunity too good to pass up. Mr. Foiles, if I could make contact with him, would be only about an hour's drive away, and his signature would make a great addition to that '55 Indians team ball. So the time came for me, once again, to be boldly spontaneous.

My sleuthing began with a search for phone numbers for financial service firms in the Norfolk area. After placing three attempts, I was able to locate someone who provided me with the company name and phone number for Mr. Foiles' office. In just a few minutes, I had him on the line.

Immediately, I found Mr. Foiles to be amiable and amenable to listening to my proposal. "You see, Mr. Foiles," I began, "I have this baseball that has already been signed by several of your 1955 teammates. I would like your autograph, too, so I was wondering if I could drive over and meet you sometime."

"Sure, I would be happy to do that," he said. "Now, it's almost two o'clock, and I'll be here at the office until about four or so. I'll stay here until then if you can make it. The office is not hard to find, so I'll be expecting you."

After providing me with precise directions, I agreed to see him well before 4:00 P.M. With the excitement of a lottery winner, I gathered the precious baseball as well as other items for him to sign: my 1950s style Cleveland Indians cap, my 35-year-old Hank Foiles model catcher's mitt, and several pens needed for good autographs.

I arrived at the office of DBA Financial Services well ahead of my schedule, and he immediately welcomed me into his workplace and introduced me to some of his associates—one of whom was his son Marc.

Mr. Foiles willingly accommodated me with the autographs, carefully applying his signature on the ball directly below that of his old friend and roommate Herb Score. Score had the honor of being voted the American League's Rookie of the Year for 1955.

"Yeah, Herb and I roomed together after he first got called up to Cleveland. We were pretty good friends. We spent some time together in the minors, too, at Indianapolis.

"Doug, your phone call has brought back so many memories. I recall traveling by train with the team when pitching star Bob Feller would often pack dumbbells inside a suitcase that would surprise unsuspecting porters grabbing the luggage handles.

"And then there was the time Bob Lemon, the Cleveland pitcher, and I were walking to the stadium. We passed an auto dealership, and Lemon went inside, made a deal and paid cash for a car. Spur of the moment! Just like that!"

I was mesmerized as this longtime hero allowed me to accompany him in his time-travel of memories.

"Bob Lemon was a great guy," he continued. "He would often spring for the check when he went out to eat with some of the younger players. But Bob would caution us and say, 'Don't you fellows forget to do the same once you've been here a few years, and there's a whole new crop of rookies on the club.'"

I could have stayed for hours just listening to the stories. As I thanked him for the visit and his reminiscences, he laughed heartily and confessed that all of his stories were of things that took place long ago. "Those are the only good stories an old man like myself can tell," he joked. "And, Doug, you're not a young kid yourself, either! Anyone who got a Hank Foiles catcher's mitt for his birthday has to be getting up there in years, too!"

At that moment, his son Marc walked in with some files. "Now, just wait a minute, Dad," he interrupted. "Doug is nowhere close to being an old guy. I'll bet we are pretty close in age, and I know I'm not old!"

We shared a light laugh over Marc's claim to youth and determined that we were probably only two years apart.

"I am the old man here," Hank asserted. "That's why Marc is handling the biggest part of my clients now. I am slowly becoming less involved now, so if you should ever have a need for some help in planning your future and your retirement, Marc is a good man to see."

Good sales pitch, I thought, and something to consider.

I turned to Marc, "Maybe we should talk about this stuff sometime soon. I would like to be able to retire within the next 20 years. That means if the next two decades go as fast as the last two, then I'd better start doing a better job of planning and saving than I have so far!"

"I'd be happy to hear from you, Doug, and I'd be glad to help any way I can. Just give me a call," he said as he handed me a business card.

There are times in life when you see through hindsight that what seemed a casual encounter, a chance meeting, or a coincidental quick introduction, actually causes an auspicious impact. This would be one of those times.

Over the next several months, I started putting more thought into my financial future. Thinking how an early and comfortable retirement appealed to me, I pulled out the business card and called Marc's office. My previous experience with financial planners had made me wary since many were known to lure in the "little guys" only to abandon them later. Marc was different.

We discussed the basics and initiated a strategy about how to maximize my meager holdings. We talked IRAs, roll-overs, mutual funds, and 401k's. Over the weeks, he returned my subsequent phone calls. We met for lunch. We talked about our jobs, our families, baseball, and growing up. We learned that we shared common ground when the conversation turned to divorce, middle age, food, antiques, and religion.

Soon we found ourselves calling each other and getting together for reasons that had nothing to do with our business relationship. Our bond included our girlfriends, and we began visiting at each other's homes for cookouts and baseball games. We had become friends.

My dear friends
Marc and Sandy

Over the past few years, the nest egg has been growing. With Marc's help, my balance continues to increase. But I am richer in many other ways, too, because of my friendship with Hank Foiles' son.

Because of this special friendship, we both celebrated at each other's 50th birthday parties. In November 2002, with my dearest friends at my home, I shared scallops and crab cakes and clam chowder and a chocolate cake ablaze with candles. And true to tradition, the guests asked to visit my "Baseball Rooms," two second-floor rooms that are replete with my baseball memorabilia. While there, Marc and his girlfriend Sandy surveyed the rooms and she asked, "What about the old catcher's mitt that Hank signed for you? Marc was telling me about it. Can you let us see that?"

I quietly retrieved the mitt from the collection that constitutes my personal museum and passed it to her. "This is really something special," she remarked. "This is an official Hank Foiles model. It says so right here on the glove!"

"It sure is, Sandy," I laughed. "But what makes it really special is that I was given the catcher's mitt on my tenth birthday, back in 1962. Now, on my 50th birthday, you and Marc are here to celebrate with me. What an astonishing circle. That is what really makes this special."

Life can take some unusual and unpredictable turns in the course of forty years. But who really knows? Maybe sometimes life gives us direct paths to things that are just supposed to be.

There is an old saying, "A man has wealth as long as he has one true friend." That sounds okay to me. And Marc, I consider you to be a true friend. But you still need to keep working on that nest egg!

CHAPTER 8

Ted Sepkowski

"Youth is the life of baseball—and we can't keep our youth forever."

-Babe Ruth, 1928

Ty Cobb was amazed when he learned the young player had no previous pro experience. "He's remarkable," observed Cobb, who then added, "I like him at the plate."

This impressive youngster was instantly picked out of the lineup of the International League Baltimore Orioles by the then 54-year-old "Georgia Peach" as he surveyed the team of minor league hopefuls. It was the spring of 1942. The flashy teenage second baseman who evoked this praise from the great Ty Cobb was Theodore Walter Sepkowski.

Ted Sepkowski was a husky, muscular 18-year-old, a local boy of Baltimore. The son of Polish parents, his father died when Ted was just a few months old and his mother could neither read nor write English. Ted had no easy road growing up in Baltimore. He was well known around the city as a star athlete at Mount St. Joseph's High School in Irvington. But the source of the muscular physique was hard physical work. He polished automobiles and shoveled coal to pick up a few extra few dollars to ease the financial situation of his family, which numbered 14 in all.

Ted dreamed of playing major league baseball all through his youth.

"He has the ideal arm and ideal throw for a second baseman," was the appraisal of Hall of Fame slugger Bill Terry when he observed Sepkowski working out as an 18-year-old. It was Shag Shaughnessy, President of the International League, who touted Ted as a $50,000 prospect after his first few games as an Oriole. But it was the good fortune of my beloved Cleveland Indians to have a working agreement with the Orioles in the early 1940s. At this time, ongoing dealings involving players' contracts and cash deals between the major league club in Cleveland and the minor league Orioles had left the Indians with an advantage. An agreement between the clubs called for the Tribe to be permitted to pick any two prospects of their choice from the Baltimore roster at the cost of just $10,000 each. Chief Wahoo, the wide-grinning, toothy, cartoon logo of the Indians was given reason to smile even bigger when Cleveland selected Sepkowski as one of their "steal of a deal" choices, a $50,000 rookie for just ten grand!

Soon after his promotion to the Indians, Ted got his first sweet taste of baseball at the major league level. But, as was the case with all healthy, young American males of the period, the harsh reality of World War II was weighing heavily on the heart and mind of Ted Sepkowski. He got a quick trial of just ten at-bats as an Indian late in the season, before he got "the call" from his most demanding yet deserving relative, Uncle Sam.

Ted helped to protect the country for two years by serving in the United States Coast Guard in 1944 and 1945. He returned to the Cleveland Indians in 1946 after another brief stint in the minors, this time at Oklahoma City. He discovered that Cleveland had a traffic jam of players competing for jobs around the infield after the war. There had been seven Indian infielders who had their baseball careers interrupted by World War II, not including their player-manager shortstop Lou Boudreau.

Ted saw action in only three games with the Tribe in '46 and then it was back to the minors again. He was dealt to the talent-laden New York Yankees in 1947, where he found even fewer opportunities. The Yankees were world champions that season but hardly due to Ted's contributions. He appeared in just one game as a Yankee and the book was then closed on his career in major league baseball.

He continued to earn his livelihood in pro baseball for several more years. Ted was employed by various teams to work as a coach and instructor in their farm systems and eventually managed minor league clubs for the Milwaukee Braves and Washington Senators. After his baseball years, Ted settled into a much more conventional lifestyle and worked as a newspaper circulation sales manager for the publishers of the *Baltimore Sun* and *The Evening Star*.

The first time I spoke with Mr. Sepkowski was by phone in the spring of 2001, after locating him in Severna Park, Maryland, by calling long distance information and taking the chance to speak with a man who is among a select group I hold in high regard: those men who once wore the uniform of the Cleveland Indians.

"Ted is out back in his shop doing some woodworking," his wife said when she answered my call. "Give me a minute to go get him. He won't mind at all."

On the phone, Ted seemed happy to speak with someone who knew about him as an ex-ballplayer. "Yes, Doug, I was out back doing some piddling. I like working with wood, and I'm working on a display case with a glass front panel. Just staying busy."

Though very congenial, Ted was difficult to understand, which I soon learned was attributed to some recent surgery for oral cancer—the result of many years of chewing tobacco. A portion of his tongue had been removed, and he would be losing several teeth because of radiation treatments. In spite of his situation, however, he projected a positive outlook. "I'm going to do fine now, Doug," he said. "My speech will get better with time, and they can replace my old teeth with new ones."

I told Ted about my collecting interests and that I had several items related to the '46 Indians that I wanted him to see and autograph for me. He was receptive to my idea to pay him a visit, and we settled on a day later in the week.

The trip turned out to be a three-hour drive north to Severna Park, Maryland, a heavily populated area spotted with businesses as well as numerous neighborhoods and residential developments. The winding roads that led to a grid of quiet side streets proved a navigating challenge, but after solving the geographical puzzle, I arrived at Ted's home, much to the credit of his precise directions.

Ted and his wife Marguerite lived in a well kept, modest neighborhood of tree-lined streets and shade-dappled yards. The Sepkowski's yard was in full bloom with colorful azaleas and daffodils.

Ted welcomed me and after quick introductions and a handshake, I was immediately led to the basement. This part of the house was obviously all Ted's territory. He was eager to show his own collection of mementos which he had saved from his 15 years in pro baseball. He had bats, caps, and signed photos and balls arranged for exhibit. Not just limited to his collection, his pride extended to the wooden shelves, the bat rack, the small display cases, and even a heavy wooden bar, as well as the other pieces that made up his private shrine to baseball.

Ted's status as an accomplished woodworker was evident in all of these furnishings he had made using stained wood, felt, Plexiglass, and brass trim. On the walls, were photographs trimmed with sturdy, high-quality frames he had crafted in his backyard shop just weeks before. Ted was particularly proud of some of those same photos. They pictured him in uniform, posed with some of the great Indian players from the '40s—men who, at one time, were his teammates: Lou Boudreau, Joe Gordon, Ken Keltner, Bob Feller, and other Cleveland Indian notables.

In spite of the effort he had to put forth to speak clearly, he enjoyed conducting this tour through his memorabilia and reliving this part of his past, a time when he was stronger and healthier. At one point during the visit, Ted's voice became somber and he said, "Doug, I had a lot of wonderful times in baseball. Even though my career was cut short by the war, or by my lack of ability, or whatever, I had a great time and I wouldn't trade it for anything. But, I have one huge regret about that period of my life."

I turned to look at him and said, "Sir?"

Ted's eyes glistened. "I wish I had stayed away from tobacco. You know, chewing tobacco. They call it 'spit-tobacco' today, but it's all the same. I tell you, my life would be a lot more pleasant now if I had not taken it up. It was something that a lot of us were doing while we were playing, but it turned out to be a very hard habit to break."

Attempting to change the subject, I said, "Well, what about a couple of autographs for me? I have a few things I have brought with me that are just begging for you to sign."

Ted seemed to snap his thoughts back to the present as he smiled, "Sure, Doug! Absolutely! I can still enjoy doing that, can't I?"

While taking a seat at this desk nearby, he explained how special and meaningful it was for him to get autograph requests in the mail. "I just can't figure it out," he confessed. "It's been over 50 years since I played my last game, and I still get two or three letters each week from people who want my autograph. They are all too young to have seen me play, and if they say they remember me, they are probably lying. Their dads might have seen me play but not the people who are doing the collecting today. That's why I had these little pictures printed, so I'd have a little something to sign and send back. It's funny that I get asked for my autograph now more than I did in the old days. Maybe it's because I'm one of the few guys left from the old days! I don't know."

Anticipating the long drive home, I gathered the items I had brought as well as some additional pictures Ted had autographed and given me. As we started up the stairs, I heard someone arriving at the kitchen door. "That's Mimi," Ted exclaimed "She's back. What good timing! Now you can meet her before you leave."

Charming and gracious, Marguerite smiled as we were introduced. "Call me Mimi," she insisted. "Marguerite is my real name, but all my friends and people around here know me as Mimi. And, Doug, I hope you've enjoyed visiting Ted this afternoon, because he said you were coming to talk about baseball. If that is what you have been doing, I know Ted has enjoyed himself."

"That's the truth," I confirmed. "It's been a truly memorable afternoon for me, one I'll never forget. Now, I have a favor to ask of you, Mimi, before I go. I brought along my camera, hoping you would snap a picture of Ted and me. Would you mind?'

Ted posed beside me, putting his arm around my shoulder as if we were the best of longtime friends, and Marguerite took the photograph.

"It's been great, folks," I announced. "Thank you for everything. And now I have a long drive ahead of me."

Ted walked with me to the driveway. "I look forward to your visiting again, Doug," he said with a hint of exhaustion.

"I'll be back for sure."

Driving home, I realized a new friendship was kindled that day. Soon after, we began exchanging letters and had numerous phone conversations. And I did return to Severna Park a few weeks later. What a surprise to discover in December that I had made Ted's Christmas card list. It would be later that I learned just how special Christmas was to him.

I also would learn that Ted's health was eroding much faster than any of us expected. God only gives us today with no promise of tomorrow.

Ted Sepkowski, Cleveland Indians-1946

CHAPTER 9

Ted's Christmas Letter

"If you knew who walked beside you, at all times, on this path that you have chosen, you could never experience fear again."
-- Dr. Wayne Dyer

The snow was accumulating quickly as I gazed out the office window one morning in the spring of 2002. All of the ballplayers were in training camps in Florida or Arizona, as the Grapefruit and Cactus Leagues were well underway. But here in Virginia, baseball and warm temperatures could only be imagined. Some of our talk around the water cooler was about baseball, simply because of the calendar, not the thermometer.

It was late March. I had had enough of winter. Concentrating on my job was almost impossible. I felt as if I were overdosing on cold weather and dark, dreary days. A small slice of baseball was all I would need to jumpstart my own personal spring thaw. Trying to limit my day dreaming and look busy at my desk, I was unaware that I was about to be caught off base. My morning would only get darker.

I decided to place a phone call to my friend Ted Sepkowski. Since he was a former baseball player, Ted would always be good for a short story about his experiences on the diamond or for his opinionated assessment of the current Baltimore Orioles. A brief chat with him would surely dispel my winter blues.

As was so often the case, Ted's wife Mimi answered the phone. Naturally, the first topic of the conversation was about the dreadful weather. According to Mimi, the same winter storm system that we were experiencing in Virginia had struck Eastern Maryland several hours earlier.

"Doug, it is really nasty up here," she reported. "Annapolis already has about three to four inches and the roads are pretty bad. I don't expect to be going out anywhere for the next couple of days."

Understanding the situation, I agreed. "That's probably best," I said. "Just stay home and keep warm and let the crazy people be the ones to go out in it," I suggested, and she agreed.

"Well, it's good to speak to you, Mimi," I said, "but, with all the snow and ice, I know Ted must be around the house tinkering with something. How about letting me speak with him for a few minutes?"

There was a long pause. The unexpected silence was disturbing. Then Mimi finally spoke, "Oh, Doug, I'm sorry. I thought you would have known by now." Again, there was a pause as she struggled to find her next words. "Doug, Ted passed away. It's been about three weeks now." Again silence. "I guess I thought that you would have seen it in the newspapers or would have heard by now," she said apologetically.

I was stunned.

"I should have called you," Mimi continued. "I'm sorry. Now that I think about it, I'm sure it wasn't in the papers down in your area."

Hearing her words but not wanting to accept them, I was overwhelmed by how surreal the conversation was. "Mimi, I am so sorry," I finally responded. "No, I didn't have any idea. The last time I spoke to him on the phone he seemed to be fine. I am so sorry to hear this."

Realizing how upsetting the news of Ted's death was for me, Mimi quickly became the consoler. "Doug, Ted and I had 55 wonderful years together and it all ended so suddenly. We were always very close to each other, as you could probably tell. And he thought a lot of you, too, Doug. He considered you to be a new friend, but a good one."

After hanging up the telephone, I sat at my desk trying to collect my thoughts and digest the bad news I had just received. I needed to share this with someone. But who? I walked slowly over to the windows and looked out toward the parking lot where, by now, everything was obscured beneath deep drifts of snow.

A few days later I received a large envelope in the mail from Mimi. She had sent copies of Ted's obituary, along with a copy of a recent issue of the *Baltimore Sun*, featuring an in-depth article about his career. An accompanying recent photograph pictured Ted posing proudly in his trophy room.

Mimi continued to stay in touch. Through letters and telephone calls, we kept each other apprised of the events in our lives, all the while becoming close friends as well.

The seasons changed and as the end of 2002 loomed, I realized that the upcoming holiday season would be Mimi's first Christmas without Ted.

Or would it be?

I called her at the start of the holidays and learned that her Thanksgiving had been a pleasant one with family. She explained how they all missed Ted so very much, but several relatives had recalled fond memories of him. Mimi was thus finding comfort with her family and friends, but as expected, I could tell she was still concerned about how to navigate her way through the holidays at home alone for the first Christmas in over a half century.

"Ted just loved Christmas," she explained. "He enjoyed all of it so much. He enjoyed the family and the children and the grandchildren—the decorating and the food." She paused for a few seconds, as if not sure about bringing something different into the conversation.

"Doug, I have something to tell you about. It's a little strange, but I want to share it with you. Just a day or two ago, I was in the living room, straightening up a few things and contemplating Christmas and trying to decide how much decorating, if any, I would do. For some unknown reason, I pulled open a drawer in a wooden table there in the living room. Don't ask me why. This drawer is usually empty, and I expected it to be then. Inside, I found a letter, a letter from Ted, one he had written many years ago.

"Doug, I have always kept all of the letters Ted wrote to me back in my bedroom closet, bound with string and stored in a box, so I don't know why this one would be separate from the others. I read the letter and found it was from the forties, before we were married. It was written at Christmastime, and Ted was telling me in the letter how he couldn't wait to be with me at Christmas, and how we would always be together at Christmastime, every year from now on.

"And that's not the end of it," she confided. "Not long after that incident, I walked from the back door onto the porch to go outside, and there, lying on the porch floor, directly in the place where you would normally step, was Ted's favorite Christmas ornament! It's a small baseball Santa Clause that he always hung in a special place on our tree each year. I can't explain how it ended up there since there were no other decorations kept out there, and who would have dropped it or placed it there?"

Mimi continued to explain how these strange happenings first startled her and were even scary at first. But after assessing the situation carefully, she determined that if, in fact, they are some sort of signs or messages, then who would want to send them? Wouldn't they be intended with love?

"After all," she concluded, "he loved me while he was here, so why would he stop now?"

She was beginning to find comfort in all that had happened, and I was pleased to think that Mimi would share such personal experiences with me, which has made me more aware of just how big of a role trust plays in a friendship.

Over the next two years, I remained in touch with Mimi. I even had the opportunity for several visits in 2003, while traveling through Maryland with some friends. We were welcomed at her home as if we were family. But, all too often, we see how life can sometimes be cruel to the kindest people.

When I phoned Mimi just after New Year's Day 2005, it was easy to tell by her voice that all was not right.

"We haven't talked in a while, Doug, so I need to catch you up on what's been going on. Back in the fall, I was diagnosed with cancer, and it's been pretty rough on me. I was undergoing treatments of chemo and radiation, and they made me so sick! Well, I have decided to stop all of that. My decision to do that was certainly against what my doctor suggested, but I was feeling so bad, and I realized that this sort of life is not *living.* So, at this time, I do not receive any of those treatments, and I have put it all in the hands of the One who is really in control of the situation. I have decided to go in this direction and pray that God will do what's best." Her voice projected courage and faith and resolve, but also exhaustion. It was easy for me to tell that Mimi had just recently made the most difficult decision of her life.

"Doug, I don't want to have to tell you all of these negative things, but I feel you are a dear friend, and you should know," she added.

What a way for her to start the new year, I thought. While the outlook of Mimi's situation did not appear hopeful, I kept her in my prayers. Still, even my own faith was faltering.

I had more to learn.

In February, I tried to phone Mimi to stay in touch, but I got no answer. Again, in March I called. No answer. By now I was imagining the worst. Was she at home and unable to pick up? Was she hospitalized? Was she in the care of family? With mounting concern, I tried calling twice more in April. It was then that I got the most surprising of answers, an answer not just to the phone call, but more important, an answer to prayers as well.

"Hello, Mimi? Is that you?"

I was incredulous. Her voice was strong and familiar. "Yes, Doug, it is. How are you?" she asked.

"Mimi, I'm fine, but what about you? I haven't been able to contact you for so long, and I've been concerned about you. Fill me in. Are you all right?"

"Yes, I'm doing well. I got some really good news about two or three weeks ago."

A wave of relief washed over me as I anticipated the details.

"At my last visit to the oncologist, for a follow-up, he told me that he could find no signs of cancer anywhere! He said the tumor I had is completely gone." Silently, I sent up a prayer of gratitude and joy as she continued. "And that's not all, Doug. I had lost about 33 pounds because of all of this, and now I have put about 20 of those back on!"

"That's wonderful news!" I exclaimed. "That's the best we could have hoped for."

"It sure is wonderful news to me," she agreed. "And the doctors are all surprised at what happened. But you know, Doug. I believe I had so many people pulling for me and praying for me, that something good had to come out of all of this."

"That's the truth, Mimi. Miracles still do happen, and you are blessed and loved and protected."

The next day I sent Mimi a letter. It was my way to continue to share the joy of her miraculous recovery. In it I started with the opening of the Doxology,

Dear Mimi,

    Praise God, from whom all blessings flow!

My young friend Rose and I visit Mimi Sepkowski
at her home in Severna Park, Maryland - 2003

CHAPTER 10

"High Pockets"

"The world does not require so much to be informed as reminded."
-- Hannah Moore

George "High Pockets" Kelly shown here in a New York Giants' uniform also spent time with the Brooklyn Dodgers.

He played baseball in a different time—a time when the terms *artificial turf, designated batter,* and *free agent* were never mentioned. It was a time when players had winter jobs for five or six months each year to supplement the meager salaries they earned as major leaguers. As sports writer, Dick Draper, once wrote, "They were good old days when they (the players) had nicknames, not agents."

His name was George Lange Kelly. His nickname was "High Pockets." Kelly was a powerful right-handed batter. At 6 feet 4 inches, he was also one of baseball's brightest stars during the sport's golden era of the 1920s and 30s. As a first baseman for the New York Giants, he played an important role for the team, which captured the National League championship four years in a row, 1921-1924. It was during this period of National League dominance that the Giants were World Champions twice, defeating the powerful New York Yankees and Babe Ruth in the World Series of 1921 and 1922.

While The Babe posted incredible marks for offensive production during the decade of the 20s, George Kelly launched his own name into the ranks of the notable sluggers by topping the senior circuit in home runs in 1924 and in runs batted in for two other seasons.

It was in August 1973, when the local newspaper here in eastern Virginia ran a feature article in the sports section. The headline read "Long Wait Is Over with Immortality for Baseball Star George Kelly." The AP story related how just a few days earlier Kelly had been inducted into the National Baseball Hall of Fame in Cooperstown, New York. Now, after spending a few days in Cooperstown participating in press conferences and photo shoots, he was on base at the nearby U.S. Naval Weapons Station in Yorktown, Virginia. There, he was visiting his daughter and son-in-law before returning to his home in Melbrae, California.

After reading, digesting, and pondering the story, I began to scheme. I considered the fact that this naval base was only a ten-minute drive from my home. I thought about the thrill of seeing this newly named member of the Hall of Fame in person. Would he be accessible? How long would he be around town? A myriad of questions popped up all at once. I found myself easily discouraged, however, especially when I expressed my hopeful intentions to a few of my friends.

"Are you really serious?" was the prevailing response, coupled with remarks of doubt and caution such as, "You can't get onto the base—you're a civilian. You'll need press credentials."

Because I heard all of this as the voice of reason, and because, at 20, I was less inclined to try the unconventional than I am now, I opted for the more reasoned tack: I waited.

And waited.

It was four or five years later that I happened upon Mr. Kelly's home address, which was listed in a sports hobby magazine along with addresses of other former athletes who were known to respond favorably to collectors seeking autographs. I wrote a concise letter explaining how I had wanted to meet him and get his signature years earlier when he was in Yorktown, just minutes from my neighborhood.

Mr. Kelly promptly replied, sending several signatures on 3 x 5 index cards, as well as a signed Hall of Fame postcard of himself, which he supplied.

I never had the pleasure of meeting Mr. Kelly. He passed away in 1984 at the age of 89 in Burlingame, California. Many years have passed since his publicized family visit to Virginia. The yellowed newspaper clipping announcing the occasion and the autographs he sent are framed and have been displayed as part of my collection for many years. There have been many instances when I have recalled George and thought about how fortunate I am, as a collector to own his coveted signature. Along the way, I have accumulated other pieces of "Kellybilia," including a few old picture-cards, several signed personal and legal documents, his lapel ribbon worn during Hall of Fame ceremonies, and my favorite item: a copy of Stan Musial's biography, *The Man, Stan Musial*, personally signed by "Stan, the Man" to his friend, George. The book is also signed by the author, Pete Broeg, and by George L. Kelly himself!

These mementos have provided a small look into the personal and professional aspects of Kelly's life. Items such as insurance papers, loan applications, and land development agreements can give insight about the responsible attention a man directs toward his financial affairs and the security of his family.

And what about his family? Could it be that he still had relatives in my area? Not likely. It was 1973 when I first learned his daughter was living on base as active military. And how could I trace the whereabouts of her family? I would not know where to begin my investigating since I did not have any basic facts to work with, not even a name. If his daughter married, she would no longer be a Kelly. Also, by this time, she and her husband were probably retired from the navy and would have likely moved.

Currently, all major league players have agents and very few of them have nicknames. With the average salary at almost $3 million a year, not one has to work a winter job just to make ends meet.

Life is different in my world. I was laboring at my desk, giving my company my best in 2005, when I received a phone call, an enlightening connection that prompted the realization of how small this world really is. It was also a confirmation that those unexpected connections made in our lives are sometimes pre-aligned.

The caller was a longtime friend, Tom Taylor, a co-worker in a former job from years earlier. In those days, we were often assigned to the same projects, and sometimes we would get together after work to share some food or to attend a ballgame.

This time he was calling to give me the name that his daughter Caroline had mentioned in some recent conversations about her fiancé's family. The wondrous part is that Caroline's future mother-in-law is Patricia Kelly Shermer, daughter of George L. "Highpockets" Kelly!

Tom continued to say that he had spoken to Mrs. Shermer about me, about my collection of baseball memorabilia, and how the collection included several pieces that related to her father's career.

"This lady is anxious to meet you, Doug, and to see your collection," Tom said. "She is going to call you soon, or you can give her a call first, if you want."

The idea of waiting was too much for me to consider, and I had that prevailing feeling that something that was once so remote was suddenly within my grasp.

Within minutes of talking with Tom, I dialed the number, and I was greeted by the cheerful, energetic Mrs. Shermer. I introduced myself, and she immediately acknowledged my connection to Tom.

"Yes, Doug, I know who you are. Tom has told me about you, and I understand you have a lot of my father's things. I'd love to meet you and see the collection sometime."

Her congeniality over the phone was striking, and her enthusiastic interest was flattering. To be honest, I did not expect her to be so receptive. After all, this is the daughter of a superstar athlete, a Hall of Fame baseball player. I had the preconceived notion that Pat, or anyone else with a family of such celebrity, would be weary of the questions and the accompanying attention.

That was not the case with Pat. During our conversation, I told Pat about my vivid recollection of her father's visit 32 years earlier and about the framed newspaper article.

"You're kidding!" she said in disbelief. "That's incredible."

I continued with my inventory of autographs and other items, and she again seemed impressed. "I'm glad to know someone like you, Doug, who has knowledge about my dad and has taken such an interest in him and his career."

It was clear that Pat enjoyed talking about George and that she was proud to be his daughter. She invited me to visit one day after work to see her own collection of old photos and to peruse her scrapbook—all related to George's baseball days. Trying to restrain my excitement, I accepted the invitation and planned to visit the next afternoon.

As I left the office that day, a cold, steady drizzle fell, making rush hour traffic stall. However, I eventually arrived at the Shermer home, a modest rancher in a quiet residential section of York County, Virginia. Their house was the epitome of genuine and unpretentious family atmosphere. Tom, Pat's husband, was reclining in front of the TV, recuperating from a bout with the flu and watching the local news broadcast. The grandchildren, who had just arrived from school, energized the atmosphere as they scurried around.

Pat immediately called my attention to several pictures hanging in the hallway on our way to the living room. They were all of George during his playing and coaching career. One notable photograph was from the 1924 World Series capturing George as he crossed home plate after hitting a home run against the Washington Senators' great pitcher Walter Johnson.

"You, know," I said, "when George was a New York Giant, he and his team had quite a strong rivalry with Washington back in the 20s."

Pat smiled and said, "With you here, Doug, I'll have the chance to learn more about these old photos because a lot of them were taken before my time. You need to keep in mind that I didn't come along until the latter part of Dad's career, so you tell me all you can about the old stuff. I'm much too young to know about some of this," she laughed.

Pat led me to the dining room table, all the while toting a large brown scrapbook under her arm. "There are several pictures in here that I think you'll enjoy," she said, pointing to the album. "Some of it is baseball, some of it is just family. There are even a few variations of his obituary in here. Just take your time and enjoy."

As I thumbed through the pages, Pat shared some insightful stories of what life was like growing up as the daughter of George "High Pockets" Kelly.

"He loved us children dearly—all three of us. I remember the wonderful breakfasts he cooked. He would cook pancakes and eggs and oatmeal for us. And he was always the teacher. He wanted us to know about things and experience life. That's why he was always taking us places like the zoo or museums or factories, just to learn and see how things are done."

We continued our journey through the picture album and stopped at another stunning snapshot. "See, that's me looking through the telescope. That's Dad pointing off in the distance, telling me what I should be seeing. He was always my teacher."

I flipped through countless pictures from family gatherings, Christmases, and George with his wife Helen. There were school pictures of the children and photographs of the children with the family pets.

"Oh, Doug, that one is our pet pig Cracker! He was such a nice pig. He was being raised to be slaughtered and we wanted to save him, so we talked Dad into letting us take him home. He helped us raise Cracker who lived to be a very old pig! My dad always helped and supported us in all of our interests and activities. I have such great memories of him. He was a wonderful father."

"What about baseball, Pat?" I asked. "Was that an activity for you and the family?"

"No, not really. He encouraged us to play sports if we chose. But it wasn't something that was expected of us. Now, he did enjoy taking us to the ballpark. Later in his career, he was a coach for the Oakland Oaks of the Pacific Coast League. He would take me and my brother Walter with him. He would have to get there really early, long before game time to do his work.

"We would bring along our own hot dogs from home, take them to the concession stand for the workers to pile on mustard and ketchup, and then eat them there at the stadium before the game. The workers didn't mind because we were George Kelly's kids!"

"So, Pat," I interrupted again, "it seems that everyone knew who George was and that must have given you a special feeling when he was recognized."

"Sure. Everyone seemed to know him, but it wasn't like we were mobbed or anything like that. People always called him by name whenever we went about town."

"Tell me about your father's name, Pat." I was curious about his famous nickname. "Was he referred to as George? Or did people call him High Pockets?"

"It almost always was George or Mr. Kelly. We didn't hear 'High Pockets' very often."

Patricia Shermer and her son, Tommy come to visit and see my collection, which includes many items that once belonged to her dad.

Then Pat offered even more background. "Do you know where the name 'High Pockets' came from?" she asked.

"Not really," I confessed. "I assume it came from his physical height, since he was one of the tallest players of his time at 6 feet 4 inches."

"Yes, that's true, Doug. But, as the story goes, it was when he was touring Japan with the All-Star team from the U.S. back in the '20s. It seems that many of the American players were purchasing dress suits and having them custom tailored while there because the suits were so inexpensive. One Japanese tailor remarked about my dad's trousers, saying that the legs were so long.

"'These pants go with suit for Mr. High Pockets,' the tailor declared. Everyone laughed and the name just seemed to stick from then on."

Sensing a candor in Pat, I felt confident and comfortable talking with her, comfortable enough, in fact, to ask something probing and personal. "Tell me, Pat, was George a religious man? I have a feeling that he was."

"Well, we were raised in the Catholic Church and our parents always had us attend church regularly. But, Dad was more than just religious. He was religious as far as going to church on Sunday. But it didn't stop there. He was a spiritual man all week long, every day.

"Doug, it was not unusual for me as a young girl to walk down the hallway at home and pass by his bedroom. The door to his room would be just partially open. I would pause and look in and see him kneeling beside the bed in prayer."

Such was a daughter's testimony to the decency, character, and spirituality of her father, George L. Kelly.

"Well, the hour is late, and I need to be going, but I hope you will come to my home for a visit and see the collection," I said, getting up to leave.

Pat followed me to the walkway, then stood in the soft rain and said, "Thank you for coming, Doug. I would very much like to see your baseball treasures. You know what? This was very special for me, and I know he must be looking down, smiling at what just happened here today."

"You're right, Pat. I have no doubt about that. And I'm sure he must be smiling!"

Christmas at the Kelly's home during the 1940s, Pat is at
far right next to her famous father.

CHAPTER 11

Bennie Huffman—Few Are Chosen

"You see, you spend a good piece of your life gripping a baseball; and in the end it turns out that it was the other way around all the time."

- Jim Bouton

Young Bennie Huffman - with the elegant,
interlocking letters S, T, L on his cap

Fifty-six games out of first place!. . . An incredible distance from the top team in the league to last place. But that is precisely the position that the St. Louis Browns found themselves in at season's end in 1937. The team completed the bleak campaign with just 46 victories stacked against 108 defeats. The Browns were struck with financial problems throughout the team's history, and it was never more evident than in 1937. They hired Rogers Hornsby and Jim Bottomly, a couple of the game's brightest luminaries, to be field managers and to play an occasional game. St. Louis management hoped that the reputations of these two baseball immortals would bolster their sagging attendance, thus providing some much needed capital. But "Rajah" and "Sunny Jim" did little to remedy the situation. Each of them had long passed their glory days and could do little to get the attention of sports fans in St. Louis. The Browns continued to stay behind in paying their bills, doing poorly at the gate, as well as on the field.

The teams also tried another avenue in an attempt to escape the cellar of the American League. They searched the country for the youngest prospects, those with the most talent, many just leaving high school, those who had yet to get attention of scouts from other clubs. This would be an extensive hunt for talent in its rawest of forms. This diamond-in-the-rough, needle-in-a-haystack approach was seen as a possible way for the Browns to find a bargain player for the future if their shoestring budget would allow them one. Their all out search for young talent was implemented by conducting huge try-out camps, the most prominent being Rogers Hornsby's Baseball Camp in Hot Springs, Arkansas, in the spring of 1937. The tryout was attended by more than 400 hopeful young men, and the scenario was reminiscent of the biblical verse: "Many are called, but few are chosen."

Among the few was a 22-year-old catcher named Benjamin Franklin Huffman. Research of record books shows that Huffman suddenly appeared on the Browns' major league roster that year. The numbers he posted were quite impressive for a young rookie. Yet, he seemed to disappear from the "big show" just as quickly as he arrived. Surely an organization in desperate need of a young prospect would have reserved a place for Huffman. But, he had only the one season in the majors. The story behind the story is what I hoped to hear when I first contacted Bennie in the spring of 2003.

Knowing that Mr. Huffman was a native of Virginia and still resided in the Commonwealth, I decided to try to arrange a trip to his hometown of Luray to meet and visit with the then 88-year-old ex-catcher. To get things started, I spoke with my good friend Jerry Varner at church. Jerry had grown up in Luray and remembered Mr. and Mrs. Huffman from his younger days. He agreed to check with a few of his old friends from back home to see if the Huffmans were still living there in town and if their health was such that they would be amenable to receiving visitors. Jerry got back to me right away with a phone number and an address.

After placing the call, I immediately felt at ease by Mrs. Huffman's soft voice. "Yes, that's right. My husband Bennie played baseball a long time ago. I would put him on the telephone, but his hearing is so bad now that you would have a lot of difficulty trying to talk. He does so much better when he talks with someone in person, and he just loves to talk about baseball!"

Mrs. Huffman gave me the impression that she would go to great lengths to accommodate someone, even a stranger. "If you could come by," she continued, "he would enjoy talking with you. But, you should probably wait until the snow goes away. Just give us a call before you come, and it will most likely be okay because we don't usually go out very often."

That spring snow in the Virginia mountains melted a few days later, and I telephoned Mrs. Huffman again. This time she agreed that a visit the next day would be fine. After giving me directions to their home, she said she and Bennie would be expecting me shortly after lunch.

A cold April drizzle fell relentlessly during the four-hour trip to Luray, but I made good time in spite of the weather until I reached the higher altitudes of the Virginia Blue Ridge. Once there, I was challenged to navigate the ribbon of road threading through the mountains that were shrouded in heavy fog. The poor visibility forced me to reduce my speed to a crawl. I was finally relieved to reach the outskirts of town, just as the fog lifted. And I still arrived ahead of schedule

I decided to explore the area and discovered Luray was a busy, little mountain city during the weekday lunch hour. The main street was a long stretch spanning from one hill to the next with signs indicating that Luray Caverns was still a popular attraction.

This day, however, did not appear to be a day for tourists in Luray. I found a fast food restaurant and ate in my car while I reviewed the notes about the Browns of 1937 that I had jotted down the previous night.

When I arrived at the Huffman home, Bennie himself greeted me at the front door. His wide smile and firm handshake signified the congeniality of the quintessential gentleman.

"Glad you made it. I imagine the fog on Route 211 was pretty bad for you on a day like this. Come on in, and let's sit down so we can talk," he said, eager to begin.

He led me into a large family room with a fireplace and walls of stately wood panels. In the adjacent kitchen area, Mrs. Huffman was clearing the last few dishes from their lunch. After our introductions, Mr. Huffman, insisting that I call him "Bennie," confessed that he wasn't really sure what I was interested in or what I came to talk about.

"But I pulled a few things out that you might like to see," he offered.

In the family room were two chairs positioned at the table with a stack of three scrapbooks, ready for Bennie's time travel through the past. As we started thumbing through the first of the albums, it was easy to tell that his pro career was not the only part of Bennie's baseball past that was meaningful to him.

"We had a really good team in high school," he said. "Floyd Baker and I played together right here at Luray High. Of course, Floyd was a couple of years behind me, but we were together for a while. And we beat just about every team we played!"

I recalled that Floyd Baker went on to play many years as an infielder for the Browns, White Sox, Senators, and Red Sox. He remained in the major leagues as a coach for several seasons, long after his career as a player had ended. This leaves little room to wonder how Luray High School managed to field such a dominating baseball team, when they used a lineup that featured two future big league players.

"Floyd and I were also together as teammates here in the Valley League," Bennie continued. "We played at Front Royal, Newmarket, and Harrrisonburg. We won a lot of games with those teams, too! And that's when I got noticed, when I was playing in the Valley League. A scout spoke to me after a game and invited me to Rogers Hornsby's baseball camp in Hot Springs, Arkansas. I had been attending college at Bridgewater, where I was taking economics and so forth. But I got to thinking that I wouldn't really want any job where I had to spend a lot of time behind a desk. What I really wanted to do was play ball, so I went along to the camp."

According to Mr. Huffman, there were about 400 boys at that camp, all hopeful of getting a chance to play professional baseball. This group included about 14 catchers. "So I had a lot of tough competition," he said, "but I swung a hot bat that entire spring. None of the pitchers down there could get me out! Then one night near the end of the camp, Rogers Hornsby himself called me to come to his room. He asked me, 'You like baseball a lot, don't you?'"

"I said, 'Yes, sir, I sure do.'"

"'Well, how would you like to go to spring training with the Browns?'" he asked.

"So, I went to spring training with St. Louis without any minor league experience. And I managed to stay on the big league club the whole season!" he boasted, pointing to a Browns' team photo in the scrapbook.

"My batting was drawing a lot of attention," he added. "I must have batted about .600 or .700 during the spring exhibition season, so that's why Mr. Hornsby kept me on the team. I was probably the only player from the eastern part of the United States that ever made the major leagues directly out of spring training without any time spent in the minor leagues and remained on the big club for an entire season," Bennie explained.

He turned another page in the album. We were still in the first volume, and I was momentarily captured by a close-up portrait of a very young Bennie, wearing his St. Louis uniform and cap with the elegant interlocking letters *S, T, L*. I particularly noticed the pieces of tape at each corner of the picture. The tape, now yellowed from age, was falling loose from the page, but the condition of the book did not seem to matter to Mr. Huffman who continued with his story.

"I continued to hit very well all year until I hurt my shoulder," he said. "That big first baseman from the Cleveland Indians, Hal Trosky, tried to bowl me over on a play at home plate. But I thought I was a bulldozer, and I wasn't going to let him move me. That's when I dislocated my shoulder, and it took about two years to get over that injury."

He looked at me matter-of-factly. So there it is, I thought. There's the reason his career was derailed before it ever had a chance to fully develop. Yet, that injury was not quite the end of baseball for Huffman.

After it was determined that the shoulder would require an extended time to heal, he was then dispatched to Baltimore for his first exposure to the minor leagues. "That was not a good experience for me," he confessed. "The weather in Baltimore can be pretty cold in spring and all that cold didn't help my shoulder any."

Fortunately, his stay with the Baltimore club was a brief one, and he soon found himself assigned to San Antonio, Texas. It was there that both his throwing and batting appeared to be returning to normal, and he began to feel hopeful and ready to return to St. Louis to become their starting catcher.

However, it was time again for fate to put up another roadblock on Bennie's path to a successful major league career. This time, the delay came to him by mail in the form of a notice that began, "Greetings from the President of the United States." It was his call to answer.

Bennie served in the U.S. Navy for four years, causing him to finally abandon any hopes of fulfilling his dreams of a career in the majors. "It was something I had to do," he recalled. "The conditions of the world and The War were a whole lot more important than baseball, as far as I was concerned."

While listening to his story, I appreciated the nobility in his willingness to serve his country. But, at the same time, I sensed some lingering misgivings as he continued to recall his dilemma 60 years ago.

"That was a big disappointment," he admitted. "When I was in St. Louis, I had already shown that I could out hit Rollie Hemsley, their regular catcher. He was a good catcher with a lot of experience, but I was just as good behind the plate. Matter of fact, there were several good players with that '37 club. Jack Knott was a good relief pitcher. I saw him come into a game against the Detroit Tigers, where he had the bases loaded and no outs. He put out Charlie Gehringer, Hank Greenberg, and Gee Walker in order, not allowing any runs to score."

"What about your third baseman, Harland Clift?" I asked, wanting to demonstrate some of my own knowledge of the team. "Wasn't he deserving of more recognition than he received? He always seemed to hit 18 to 20 homeruns each season."

Bennie reflected for a few seconds, and then replied, "He was a pretty good hitter, all right, and a pretty fair third baseman. But he had a 'scatter arm.' He made a lot of wild throws to first base. We were fortunate to have a guy named Harry Davis playing first who was really good at scooping bad throws out of the dirt. Now, he was a good player, too. Stinky, we called him, Stinky Davis."

"Why on earth?" I laughed. "Why would you fellows give him a nickname like Stinky?"

"Oh, I don't know," said Bennie. "But we called him that."

"Well, maybe that's something I don't really want to know about, anyway," I laughed again. "Who were some of the others you played with?"

"We had a really good centerfielder named Sam West. He was a great hitter, who had spent some time with the Senators. In left field, we had Joe Vosmik, who had good power in his bat. In right field, we had Beau Bell, who could hit a ball to right-centerfield as hard as anyone I ever saw. Remember, I was also a baseball scout for about 30 years."

Realizing Bennie had witnessed a lot of baseball from the 1930s to the present, I was prompted to ask his opinion as to who was the fastest pitcher. "Since you batted against Bob Feller during his younger days, and you saw Nolan Ryan pitch 25 years ago, and you've seen someone like Randy Johnson pitch today, tell me who delivered the most 'heat'? Who was the fastest?" I pressed.

Without hesitation, Bennie announced, "Bob Feller! I batted against Bob, and I don't believe there has been anyone since then that was as fast as he was when he was young."

Now, was this an unbiased choice? I wondered. Isn't it natural that the best always seems to come from one's own time? Yet, it is only the opinions of the elderly that we can accept as valid in such cases. After all, who else can lay claim to being an eyewitness to a Feller fastball of 1937 and then the speed of a Randy Johnson pitch many decades later?

Bennie continued to talk about how, during his brief stay in the major leagues, he produced just one home run. He expressed how some people view that as a lack of accomplishment. "To some folk," he said, "hitting just one home run is like I didn't do anything while I was up there."

"Well, too bad for those folk!" I responded with no uncertainty. "Making it into professional baseball is an accomplishment that most

American males can only dream of. Playing in the big leagues like you did is a dream come true!"

How could anyone think that way and have the right to minimize the ability or record of a professional athlete, I wondered.

Bennie was in Hot Springs, Arkansas, with 400 boys at that camp, and out of the 400, he was the only one selected to sign. His lone home run in the majors was a moment of personal pride that occurred on August 1st against the powerful New York Yankees. Huffman's victim was right-handed pitcher Spud Chandler.

"I can show you the box score from that game!" Bennie said. "It was in Yankee Stadium, and we lost to the Yankees as we so often did. But in the papers the next day, the box score listed the home runs for the game: 'Gehrig—New York, DiMaggio—New York, Huffman—St. Louis.' For one day, I guess I was in with some pretty good company, wouldn't you say?"

"Yes, you were, Bennie." And I realized it was the same for me that day. For this one day, you could say that I was in some pretty good company myself.

You were great, Bennie.

Benjamin Franklin Huffman
July 17, 1914-February 22, 2005

CHAPTER 12

Joe Sewell—He Would Always Make Contact

"For each generation, today's game becomes tomorrow's nostalgia."
- Monte Irvin in *The Ball Parks* by William Shannon

The great Joe Sewell - the most difficult batter to strikeout

    The cornerstone of my memorabilia collection is the world championship team of 1920, the Cleveland Indians. My interest in this team, the pennant race, and the eventual World Series of that year was first sparked in the late 1970s. I was intrigued immediately when I learned how the final two months of that season unfolded to become one of the most exciting in baseball history.

    The steamy heat of August was having a draining effect on all the players as the Indians were battling the New York Yankees and Chicago White Sox for the top spot in the American League. The sporting public was just beginning to hear rumors of how the most recent World Series was not quite the honest confrontation that had been sold to them. In spite of this season being the first for Babe Ruth as a Yankee, his frequent and monstrous home runs were doing little to prevent fans' interest from waning. But the late season race for the A.L. flag was heating up, nonetheless, just like the weather.

    The most tragic of all major league baseball games occurred on August 16, 1920, on a damp, overcast afternoon in New York City, where the Yankees were hosting the Indians. At that point, the Cleveland Indians held first place by the slightest of margins, making any matches between these two all the more crucial. On the hill that day for New York was side-armer, Carl Mays. Mays was a submarine-style pitcher, who used an almost underhand delivery. He was a man of questionable temperament, who seldom smiled and projected a win-at-all costs approach.

It was in the fifth inning that day with the Indians leading 3-0 when Mays pitched to the popular Cleveland shortstop Ray Chapman. Chapman was a fan favorite as well as a friend to all of his teammates. As was customary for him, Chapman crowded home plate somewhat as he settled into a crouched posture, poised for his first swing. The near-underhanded offering from Mays was extremely fast, high, and inside. The spectators watched as the pitch seemed to freeze Chapman to a point where he had no reaction to its location. They next heard a distinct, audible crack, leading many to assume the ball had contacted Chapman's bat. The ball then slowly rolled out towards the pitcher's mound. But, there would be no play on this ground ball. Ray collapsed after staggering a few steps away from the batter's box. Teammates rushed out of the dugout to give aid to their fallen friend. They quickly discovered that the ball had crushed the left side of Ray's skull. He soon lost consciousness and died at a nearby hospital the next day.

Chapman's death is the only fatality in major league history, which is the result of an on-the-field mishap. The tragedy, some thought, would surely break the spirit of the Cleveland squad. Here they were in the midst of a late-season scrap for first place, and suddenly they had to search for a replacement for their star shortstop. Finding a fill-in for "Chappie" would be difficult enough, even if they weren't grieving his loss.

But the Indians' scouting department had done their homework. The Tribe quickly summoned a young shortstop out of the University of Alabama who was at that time playing for the minor league New Orleans Pelicans. His name was Joe Sewell. Sewell had never witnessed a major league game until he reached the Cleveland club that August. However, for a small player at just five feet seven inches tall and just 21 years old, little Joe did a spectacular job for the Indians. He batted an incredible .329 for the remainder of the regular season and played a vital role in causing his team to rebound from a deep, unforeseen tragedy and win the American League pennant by two games over Chicago and three games over the Yankees. And the Cindrella-like story of the 1920 Indians did not end there. They proceeded to face the Brooklyn Dodgers, champions of the National League, in the then, best of nine games World Series.

Sewell and the Indians went on to victory by taking the series five games to two as Cleveland became World Champions for the first time in the team's history. Their only other reign as champions would be 28 years later. But, it was on October 10, 1920, during the fifth game of the World Series that some other Indian players would be heroes by stepping into the spotlight that day and calculating one of the greatest games ever in post-season play.

In the first inning, Cleveland's right-fielder Elmer Smith, swatted a spitball from Dodger pitcher Burleigh Grimes over the fence when the bases were loaded for the first-ever World Series grand slam home run. Minutes later, in the bottom of the fourth inning, the Indians' pitcher of the day, Jim Bagby, applied his bat to another of Grimes's pitches. This ball also did not land until it too was beyond the fence for what would be the first home run hit by a pitcher in a World Series game. This blow by Bagby came with two Tribe base runners aboard, further increasing the Indians' lead.

With Cleveland ahead 7-0 in the top of the fifth inning, the Indians were about to inflict even more damage upon the Dodgers. A defensive play by the Indians' second-baseman Bill Wambsganss (pronounced wambs-gance) would prove to be the knockout punch that would send Brooklyn down in series defeat. The Dodgers, sensing they were mounting their most serious threat of the game, had base runners on first and second bases with no outs when a hot line drive was struck straight up the middle of the diamond, directly over the second base bag. Wambsganss lunged quickly to his right and managed to barely snag the drive with the fingertips of his tiny glove. Corralling the ball close to his body for an out, Wamby's momentum was such that his next step placed his right foot on top of second base. This contact with the base retired the Dodger runner who had left second to advance to third base on what had appeared to be a base hit to centerfield. He was just a few steps from third when the umpire called him out.

Wambsganss stopped in his tracks when he realized he had just executed two outs by himself. It was then that Joe Sewell, the shortstop, began to yell to Wambsganss, "He's behind you! He's behind you!"

Wamby spun around only to find the Brooklyn runner who had originally taken off from first base at the crack of the bat, now standing just a few feet from second, "Standing as still as Lot's wife," it was reported. The motionless runner was dumbfounded as Wambsganss ran over in his direction and applied the tag with the baseball to complete the only unassisted triple play in World Series history! This was the grandest of the three celebrated plays of the day.

Several of the key members of that 1920 Cleveland team lived to be very old men, surviving well into the 1980s. Wambsganss, Sewell, along with Smokey Joe Wood, and pitchers Stanley Coveleski and George Uhle, to name a few. My fascination with that team of champions was enhanced by the fact that I was able to contact several of these men at a time when many of them would be able to offer their insight regarding that season. My collection of letters contains several shakily handwritten notes from these ex-Indians who answered my inquiries by mail.

But it was Joe Sewell, the tiny shortstop the Tribe acquired from the New Orleans team, that I seemed to be strongly drawn to. It was Joe with whom I was fortunate to exchange letters on several occasions. He always responded to my letters, whether I was asking a question or seeking another of his autographs with which he was very generous. He was voted into the National Baseball Hall of Fame in 1977, yet he remained a kind, grounded Southern gentleman. I so appreciate all that he did for me.

Over the years, I have collected an array of 1920s Cleveland Indians memorabilia, but the items of Joe Sewell continue to be my favorites, the dearest to my heart. I own many balls and pictures that he has signed, several letters and contracts, and a pair of his old game-worn cleats, a college yearbook of his, and many other items such as cards and buttons that bear his likeness.

Joe Sewell died March 3, 1990, at the age of 91. He will long be remembered as a member of baseball's Hall of Fame, as well as the most difficult batter to strike out in history. He somehow managed to always get his bat on the ball. He would always make contact. On the average, he fanned only once for every 62 times he came to bat. I will surely recall and always appreciate his kindness. I also believe Joe is aware of my regard and appreciation.

It was March 2001, ten years after his death, that Joe seemed to acknowledge this deep mutual admiration in a vivid and uncanny dream—the type of dream that replays repeatedly in one's mind the following day. It was the type of dream where exact words and minute details are recalled. It was like a visitation as well as a dream.

The setting is the gathering of a crowd in a large auditorium, packed with people. I am front and center, first row. Joe steps out on the stage and is introduced. He then announces that he will take questions from the audience but that he has limited time, only a few minutes. He is wearing a black suit and tie with a white dress shirt. Then in his friendly Southern accent, he points at me and says, "I'm gonna start right down here at the front with my good friend Doug Williams."

Without having raised my hand, I am the first person he selects, and immediately, an unrehearsed question rolls from my lips.

"Yes, thank you, Joe." I begin. "Years ago, you played several seasons with Tris Speaker as your manager. Did you learn anything from his coaching style that you took with you and used later in life when you became a coach?"

"Yes, I sure did, Doug," he replies. "Tris taught me to always make the opposition commit himself. Force his hand. Cause him to commit. Then react to what he does. Base your action on what he does."

What came to me was a surreal and insightful glimpse of his competitive attitude with some excellent underlying advice.

At the time of this dream, I was out of town on an extended and complicated work assignment. Strangely enough, I was in New Orleans, home of the Pelicans, where in 1920, Joe Sewell was also contacted and given his next extended and complicated work assignment—to report to the Cleveland Indians, the World Series, the Big Show.

111

Could his reply be more than just a simple answer to my question? Could it have been more than his successful game plan? Maybe it was a gift, a piece of personal advice that I could draw on later on life's path.

Thanks for everything, Joe, from me, your biggest fan.

"So, it all began with tragedy. But, for me personally, the story had a happy ending."

--Joe Sewell